P9-ASL-475

8513
EBJI 11 '69

THE ELECTORAL COLLEGE

LUCIUS WILMERDING, JR.

The
Electoral College

RUTGERS UNIVERSITY PRESS

New Brunswick   *New Jersey*

FERNALD LIBRARY
COLBY-SAWYER COLLEGE
NEW LONDON, N.H. 03257

JK
539
W64

8/82 Burgess

Copyright © 1958
by Rutgers, The State University

Library of Congress Catalogue Number: 58:6290

Printed in the United States of America by
Quinn & Boden Company, Inc., Rahway, New Jersey
Designed by Leonard W. Blizard

Second Printing

86535

IN MEMORIAM
Robert Fulton Cutting

Preface

The Federal Constitution has divided the process of electing a President of the United States into two parts: one necessary, the other contingent. In the first part, as matters now stand, the people, through the agency of intermediate Electors, arrange the candidates for President in an order of preference; in the second part, the House of Representatives chooses the President from a range of names at the top of the list of candidates furnished by the Electors. However, the eventual power of the House of Representatives is not exercised if an absolute majority of the Electors give their suffrages to the same person; in such cases the candidate who stands first on the list becomes President.

The time-table of election is established by national law. Part One begins on the first Tuesday after the first Monday in the November of every fourth year, when the qualified voters of the several states choose the presidential Electors; it continues on the first Monday after the second Wednesday in December, when the Electors meet in their respective states to cast their votes for President; and it ends on January 6, when the electoral votes are counted in the presence of the two Houses of Congress and the results are announced. Part Two, if required at all, begins on January 6 and continues until a President is chosen.

Such, in the barest outline, is the system provided for filling the most important office in the nation. It is little understood by those who operate it. A voter entering a polling booth and seeing the names of two or more candidates for President printed on his ballot, checks the name of his favorite and imagines that he has cast a direct vote for President; he forgets, or he never knew, that an apparent vote for a single man as President is a real vote for a number of men as Electors pledged to vote on a future day for a particular candidate. It seldom occurs to him that a branch of the national legislature may later be called upon to complete an election which the people have left inchoate; and, when the possibility is called to his attention, he has no idea how the work is consummated or upon what principle.

Many writers on American institutions would excuse this ignorance as immaterial. Technicalities, they say, should be left to the connoisseur. What difference does it make that the people think they are electing the President by a nation-wide popular vote? A plebiscitary presidency has in fact issued from the involved indirect procedure of the Constitution. It is more likely to confuse the voter than to enlighten him, if he is asked to look at the bizarre and mystifying forms that cover the substance of an essentially simple operation.

But in point of fact the presidency is not a plebiscitary office in any normal meaning of the term. It is true that, in effect, a plebiscite is held in each state separately; but the results of these forty-eight state plebiscites are not correctly brought into the national calculations. In translating popular votes into electoral votes no account is taken of the sentiments of divisions within a state. In making up the general aggregate each candidate is given the unanimous and undivided electoral votes of every state in which he happens to have a plurality of the popular votes; from the remaining states he is given nothing. As a consequence of this artificial and delusive system, by which in each state a large minority of the people is made precisely equal to no minority at all and a bare plurality is made equal to the whole, it can seldom happen that the real sense of the people as to the relative merits of the candidates will be rightly mirrored in the ultimate results. Even the order in which the candidates are arranged by the Electoral College must in many elections be the sport of accidental combinations.

An election by the House of Representatives is still further removed from an election by the people at large. In its composition, indeed, that body reflects the political sentiments of the nation much more accurately than the College of Electors; but the mode of voting is such as to make this advantage nugatory. The representation from each state, regardless of its size, is given one indivisible vote which it casts according to the sense of its own majority. In a system that makes Nevada the equal of New York, it must be a matter of nearly equal chance whether a minority or the majority gains the ascendancy in the Union.

There is, in truth, a disparity between the intention of the Constitution with regard to the election of the President and the practical workings of the machinery which has been devised to fulfill it. The purpose of that instrument is, and has always been, to elevate to the executive chair the man who is the choice of the majority of the people in the nation as a whole. The effect of the all-or-nothing system of distributing electoral votes among the candidates is to bring in the man who is the choice of the states in their corporate capacities, due regard being had to differences in their numbers of inhabitants. The effect of the rule of voting in the House of Representatives is to elect from a range of candidates the man who is the choice of a majority of the states considered as equal sovereignties.

To make the machinery of election more fully subserve the great object of the Constitution has long been the goal of our leading statesmen. That they have hitherto failed in their efforts is due to a variety of causes. Sometimes they have offered plans of reform, good in themselves, but wholly incapable of running the gauntlet of the constitutional amending process. Sometimes their schemes, after full discussion, have seemed insufficient to their purpose. But the great obstacle to change, especially in recent years, has always been public apathy—an apathy induced and corroborated by a false understanding of the inner meaning and practical consequences of the present arrangements.

It is the double object of this book to exhibit and explain the difficulty inherent in the existing mode of electing a President and to examine the relative merits of the various proposals for its solution that are currently before the country. These proposals, of necessity, all take the form of joint resolutions of Congress to amend the Constitution; for the rule of voting in the House of

Representatives is prescribed by the Constitution itself, and the all-or-nothing system of allotting electoral votes to the candidates is the product of the concurrent action of the forty-eight state legislatures, bodies which in this matter are wholly uncontrolled by the Constitution and not subject to control by Congress.

The scope of the book is determined by its object. The Electoral College and the House of Representatives are the two agencies that, in contemplation of the Constitution, control the subject of elections to the presidency; it is with these alone that I shall be concerned. I shall make no attempt to discuss the role played in the process of election by the nominating conventions of the great political parties. These conventions stand wholly outside the Constitution. As Rufus King once observed, no article or clause of that document authorizes or gives the slightest encouragement to measures of any sort by which a concentration of the votes for President may be effected previously to the choice of Electors in the several states. Nevertheless, such measures have always been taken—at first by congressional caucuses, nowadays by nominating conventions. These bodies, the creations of party, have in a measure assumed the direction and control of the fundamental provisions of the Constitution dealing with the presidential election. By undertaking to nominate the President four or six months before his election, they anticipate what was probably intended to be the action of the people in appointing Electors. However this may be, as a consequence of their proceedings, the election of a President is half over before it has constitutionally begun. The November voters are, in fact if not in theory, prevented from making the candidates for President. They can only, through the agency of pledged Electors, declare their relative confidence in candidates already made.

In considering the parts played in the electoral process by the Electoral College and the House of Representatives, I shall posit the existence of the nominating conventions, and I shall explain how they are influenced in the choice of candidates by the state laws regulating the mode of appointing Electors; but I shall not wrestle with the complicated problem of how far the will of the people can be made to prevail over a body of delegates most of whom would ridicule the idea that they are members for the nation and many of whom are in fact the agents for this or that special interest. The reader may satisfy himself with the pious hope that no man who is the real choice of the people can be excluded from the electoral contest in November by the action of the conventions in July.

I shall also pass over without notice the multifarious modes by which the candidates for the office of Elector are nominated in the several states. Since the Electors are agents without discretion, mere mandarin toys that nod when they are set in motion, it can make no conceivable difference how they are nominated or even who they are. It will be sufficient to say that in some states they are selected by party conventions, in others by party organizations, in still others by party primaries, and in one (Pennsylvania) by the party nominee for the office of President.

Finally, I shall omit all consideration of a problem that has formed the bulk of most previous works on the electoral system, the problem of how litigated questions are to be decided when the votes of the Electors are being counted in the presence of the two Houses of Congress. This question was formerly of great interest, but with the adoption by Congress of a law providing for every possible contingency for which the Constitution prescribes no rule, it lost most of its importance.

With respect to the College of Electors the thesis of this book may be briefly stated. It is, and was, the intention of the Constitution that the President should be chosen by the people of the United States considered as one nation. The electoral voting system was adopted instead of a direct voting system only because it seemed the most practicable way to give equal weights to equal masses of persons in a country where the suffrage laws varied widely from state to state. In committing the appointment of the Electors to the people, the state legislatures have fulfilled the intention of the Constitution; but in requiring the Electors to be appointed by a mode which gives to a single party the whole of a state's representation on the Electoral College, they have defeated that intention. They have put the presidency on a federative rather than a national basis. They have taken the choice of the President from the people of the nation at large and given it, in effect, to the people of the large states. I shall contend that the all-or-nothing system of choosing Electors in the several states is grounded on a wrong principle and that it is productive of much evil in practice.

With respect to the House of Representatives, when acting in the capacity of electors of the President, I shall relate how the framers of the Constitution themselves came to regret a rule of voting by which the smallest state is made equal to the greatest. But I shall be principally concerned to explain the regulations under which the voting has been conducted upon the two occasions when the eventual election of the President has devolved upon the House. For these regulations, were they to be followed in a modern election, would greatly hamper the reaching of a prompt and quiet decision.

In explaining the proposals for reform, I have attempted to present the arguments for and against each of them as strongly and impartially as possible. But I have not hesitated to express my own preference for a system which would not only put the election of the President on a sound theoretical basis but which would also be attended by no practical difficulties other than those which now attend the election of Representatives in Congress.

Some paragraphs of this book have appeared in the *Political Science Quarterly* and in the testimony which I have given before the House and Senate Judiciary Committees when the topic of electoral reform has been under their scrutiny.

LUCIUS WILMERDING, JR.

Princeton, New Jersey
May, 1958

Contents

Preface   vii

Part One

HISTORICAL RETROSPECT

1. The Federal Convention   3
2. The Twelfth Amendment   23
3. The Variety of Method   42

Part Two

PRESENT VIEW AND PROSPECT

4. The General Ticket Plurality System   71
5. The National Plebiscite System   95
6. The Proportional Voting System   111
7. The Single-Member District System   128
8. The Intermediate Electors   169
9. The Contingent Election   184
   Appendix   213
   Index   219

Part One

HISTORICAL RETROSPECT

1. The Federal Convention

To the members of the Federal Convention, sitting in Philadelphia during the summer of 1787, no problem appeared more difficult of solution than that of fixing the mode of choosing a President of the United States. "The subject," said James Wilson on the floor of the Convention itself, "has greatly divided this House. . . . It is in truth the most difficult of all on which we have to decide." In the Pennsylvania ratifying convention his remarks were to the same effect: "The Convention, sir, were perplexed with no part of this plan so much as with the mode of choosing the President of the United States." Nor is Wilson our only witness. In 1803, five years after Wilson's death, Senator William Plumer of New Hampshire told his colleagues that he had been "repeatedly assured, by several gentlemen who formed our Constitution, that this very subject embarrassed them more than any other—that various systems were proposed, discussed, and rejected—that the Convention were on the point of rising without being able to agree on a system to elect this high officer—that at last the principles contained in the Constitution were adopted, upon a full conviction that they were less exceptionable than any others that they were able to devise." Senator Timothy Pickering of Massachusetts, too, put in his evidence: "He had been informed by a member of that Convention, the gentleman from Georgia on his left, . . . that late in their session the present complex mode of electing the President and Vice President was proposed; that the mode was perfectly novel, and therefore occasioned a pause; but when explained and fully considered was universally admired, and viewed as the most pleasing feature of the Constitution." Pickering's neighbor on the left was Abraham Baldwin, who had been a member of the committee which devised the scheme.

That the title of the President should be elective and not hereditary was a principle accepted of course by every delegate. Reports idly circulating out of doors that the Convention intended to establish a monarchical government, to apply for a sovereign of the House of Hanover or the House of Bourbon, to invest General Washington with the prerogatives of a crowned head, were without foundation. "We never once thought of a king"—such was the uniform answer returned by the members of the Federal Convention when questioned by their correspondents on this subject. But granted that the President should be elected, by what authority should the election be made? By the national legislature? By the state legislatures or state executives? By the people? Each of these modes had vigorous adherents and equally vigorous opponents.

The advocates of an election by the national legislature were first to take the field. Everyone, they said, would agree that the executive magistracy should rest upon the great foundation of the people; but there was an immense difference between a direct and an indirect election. In a constituency as large as the United States, the people—"the well-meaning but uninformed people," as Jefferson had once called them—could have no knowledge of eminent characters and qualifications. True, there were at present distinguished citizens who were known perhaps to almost every man; but this would not always be the case. In normal times—and it is for normal times that a constitution must be made—an election by the people would be little better than an appointment by lot. "It would be as unnatural," said George Mason, summing up this part of the argument, "to refer the choice of a proper character for chief Magistrate to the people, as it would, to refer a trial of colours to a blind man. The extent of the Country renders it impossible that the people can have the requisite capacity to judge of the respective pretensions of the Candidates."

But (the argument proceeded) if the people could seldom be informed of characters in a continental constituency, they were quite competent to distinguish among their own neighbors. Let resort, therefore, be had to the policy of refining the popular appointments by successive filtrations. Let the people in their districts appoint the House of Representatives; let the House of Representatives—or, possibly, the state legislatures—appoint the Senate; and let the two Houses together appoint the Executive. The manner of making the ultimate choice—whether viva voce or by ballot—whether by joint or separate vote of the two Houses or by vote of the Senate alone from nominations made by the House of Representatives—such details could be worked out later.

Almost at once, however, the proponents of this scheme found themselves in trouble: The plan of legislative election was in apparent conflict with the principle of executive independence. The members of the Federal Convention (one or two only, excepted) considered the executive magistracy as much more than an institution for carrying the will of the legislature into effect: The President was to be the guardian of the people, their great protector against legislative tyranny. Experience had shown that public liberty was in greater danger from legislative usurpations than from any other source. Surely the President was to execute the laws, but he was also to hinder the final passage of unjust and pernicious laws, perhaps even to discourage their introduction. How could he play his part, how restrain the legislature from encroaching on the liberties of the people, unless he were independent of that body? "A dependence of the Executive on the Legislature," said Madison, "would render it the executor as well as the maker of laws; and then, according to the observation of Montesquieu, tyrannical laws may be made that they may be executed in a tyrannical manner." Mason, though a leading advocate of legislative election, was in complete agreement: "He opposed decidedly the making the Executive the mere creature of the Legislature as a violation of the fundamental principle of good Government."

In the light of these ideas, what was to be thought of the proposition that the national Executive be elected by the national legislature? Would not the Executive be the mere creature of the legislature, or rather of its predominant faction, if he were dependent upon its pleasure for an appointment? Would not the legislature and the candidates bargain and play into each other's hands? Would not votes be given by the former under promises or expectations from the latter? The difficulty would be aggravated if one of the candidates were the incumbent President. Then two evils were to be feared. Mason recognized and defined them as "a false complaisance on the side of the Legislature towards unfit characters; and a temptation on the side of the Executive to intrigue with the Legislature for a reappointment."

To get rid of these objections a proposal originally advanced as a distinct proposition was soon made part and parcel of the plan of legislative election: Let the President be appointed by the legislature, but let him be ineligible a second time. The ineligibility would prevent a complaisant legislature from continuing an unfit man in office in preference to a fit one; it would also leave the President under no temptation to court a reappointment. Once elected, the President would be free to sustain his part as *tribunus plebis*, free "to stand the mediator between the intrigues and sinister views of the Representatives and the general interests and liberties of the people."

To a great majority of the Convention, however, the idea of making the Executive ineligible a second time was, when considered solely on its own merits, extremely repugnant. In the abstract it seemed an infringement on the right of election. In practice it would produce an undesirable rotation in office and form "a political school in which we were always governed by the scholars and not by the masters." Surely, too, there was great force in Sherman's remark that "he who has proved himself to be most fit for an office ought not to be excluded by the Constitution from holding it." Besides, would the ineligibility really prevent intrigue and dependence on the legislature? If the President could not look forward to his own re-election, he would be pretty sure to look forward to the opportunity of going into the legislature itself; would he not take his measures accordingly? Worst of all, might not a constitutional bar to a re-appointment inspire in the President unconstitutional endeavors to perpetuate himself? In moments of pressing danger the tried abilities and established character of a favorite Magistrate might prevail over respect for the forms of the Constitution.

To weaken the force of these further objections the plan of legislative election was again modified: Let the President be ineligible a second time, but let his duration be lengthy, seven years at least. A long term would mitigate the evils of a rotation in office, the necessary consequence of an ineligibility. It would also bring the President to an age at which a continuance in office would cease to be agreeable to himself as well as desirable to the public.

But here again the modification was disliked by most members when viewed by itself. "Consider," said Gunning Bedford, "what the situation of the Country would be, in case the first magistrate should be saddled on it [for seven years] and it should be found on trial that he did not possess the qualifications ascribed to him, or should lose them after his appointment. An impeachment would be no cure for this evil, as an impeachment would reach misfeasance only, not incapacity." Furthermore, the notion that, at a certain advance of life, men lose either their ambition or ability, was ill-founded. Experience had shown in a variety of instances that both a capacity and inclination for public service existed —in very advanced stages. Besides, how old is old? A President might come into office at thirty-five; let his continuance be fixed not at seven but at fifteen years; at the age of fifty, in the very prime of life and with all the aid of experience, must he be cast aside like a useless hulk? And by what wonderful interposition of Providence will he at that period cease to be a man, cease to covet power and the exaltation of office?

When it became clear that a long term and a subsequent ineligibility were infrangibly attached to an election of the national Executive by the national legislature, it also became clear that this mode of election would ultimately be rejected by the Convention. The end desired could not be reached because of the incidents inseparable to it.

A second plan was projected by a group of delegates who were opposed as much to a popular election as to an election by the national legislature. An important object of the Constitution, they said, must be to preserve harmony between the national and state governments; but if these governments were to be combined in the same views and measures, the elections to the former must be made by the latter. Not only the Senate but the House of Representatives and the Executive as well should be chosen by the state authorities. The right of participation in the national government would be sufficiently secured to the people by their election of the state legislatures. In the case of the Executive, let each state be allotted a number of votes for President according to some equitable ratio; then let these votes be cast, either directly or through the agency of intermediate Electors, by the state legislatures or state executives. Such a scheme, they added, would conciliate the state partisans, who were already professing alarm that a new constitution would supersede altogether the state authorities.

The plan, however, found but little favor in the sight of the Convention. The particular states, it was pointed out, were now being asked to part with power, or as much of it as might be necessary to make a national government adequate to their peace and the security of their liberties. Would not the state governments in these circumstances be rivals and opposers of the national government? Even now, when the Continental Congress flowed (in eleven states) from the state legislatures, where was the harmony between the general and the local governments? On examination it would be found that the opposition of states to federal measures had proceeded much more from the officers of the states than from the people at large. Anyone with half an eye could see that the individual legislatures were actuated not merely by the sentiment of the people but also by an official sentiment opposed to that of the general government and perhaps to that of the people themselves. As for the state executives, notwithstanding their constitutional independence, they were in fact dependent on the state legislatures and subservient to their views. Was it likely, then, that a national Executive appointed by any branch of the state governments would defend with becoming vigilance the national rights against state encroachments?

There was also the question of bad laws. The legislatures of the states had betrayed a strong propensity to a variety of pernicious measures. One object of the national legislature was to control this propensity. One object of the national Executive, insofar as it would have a negative on the laws, was to control the national legislature, insofar as it might be infected with a similar propensity. Refer the appointment of the national Executive to the state legislatures and this controlling purpose might be defeated. The legislatures could and would act with some kind of regular plan and would promote the appointment of a man who would not oppose himself to a favorite object. Should a majority of the legislatures at the time of election have the same object, or different objects of the same kind, the national Executive would be rendered subservient to them.

These objections decided the issue. When they had been fully stated, it was plain that the advocates of an election by the state authorities could not have their way.

In the meantime the proponents of a third plan were steadily gaining ground. If, said the friends of a popular election, the President is to be the guardian of the people, let him be appointed by the people. Experience, particularly in New York and Massachusetts, had shown that an election by the people at large was both a convenient and a successful mode. If the people were to elect, they would never fail to prefer some man of distinguished character and services, some man, so to speak, of continental reputation. It had been said that such men would not be known to the people, but surely this was a mistake. If they were known to the legislature, they must have such a notoriety and eminence of character that they could not possibly be unknown to the people at large; it was inconceivable that a man should have sufficiently distinguished himself to merit this high trust without having his character proclaimed by fame throughout the empire; besides, the increasing intercourse among the people of the states would render important characters less and less unknown. It had also been said that the people, though virtuous, would be the dupes of pretended patriots, that they would be misled by a few designing men; but this too was a mistake. It might happen in particular spots that the activity and intrigues of little partisans would be successful, but the general voice of the nation could never be influenced by such artifices; the greater the constituency, the less the opportunity for demagogy.

There were two difficulties, however, of a serious nature attending an immediate choice by the people. In the first place, it seemed improbable that there would be a general concurrence of the people in favor of any one man. The people in each state would probably vote for one of their own citizens, and the largest state would have the best chance for the appointment. In the second place, the right of suffrage was much more diffusive in the Northern than the Southern states, and the latter could have no influence in the election on the score of the Negroes. Put the two difficulties together, and the large Northern states, Massachusetts and Pennsylvania, would have an advantage over all the rest. As Hugh Williamson remarked: "The people will be sure to vote for some man in their own State, and the largest State will be sure to succeed. This will not be Virginia, however. . . . Her slaves will have no suffrage."

These difficulties proved not insuperable. The first could be got over by the device of plural voting: Let each man vote for three persons as President—or, better still, for two persons, one of whom, at least, should not be of his own state; very likely, he would give his first vote to a favorite fellow citizen, but he would give his second to a continental character from another state, and continental characters were as apt to be found in a small as in a large state. Resort might also be had to the expedient used in Massachusetts, where the legislature, by a majority of voices, decided in case a majority of the people did not concur in favor of one of the candidates. If the larger states would generally have the first nomination of the persons voted for as President, the smaller states would play an important part in the eventual election.

The disadvantage to the Southern states could be surmounted by requiring the people to cast their votes through the agency of intermediate Electors. If each state were to be assigned a number of votes for President proportional to the number of its inhabitants, these votes to be cast by Electors appointed by the people, the difficulty arising from the disproportion of qualified voters in the several states would be obviated. Virginia would have the weight to which her numbers entitled her.

The mode of popular election enjoyed one advantage that was denied to other modes: It was approved in principle even by its opponents. Mason, for example, "favored the idea" of an appointment by the people, but thought it impracticable; Gerry "liked the principle" but was for waiting till people should feel more the necessity of it. Consequently, as the difficulties of this mode were shown to be susceptible of solution, it came more and more into favor. On June 1, Wilson had been "almost unwilling" to propose it, "being apprehensive that it might appear chimerical." On July 19, he "perceived with pleasure that the idea was gaining ground, of an election mediately or immediately by the people." On July 25, Madison, a convert from the scheme of legislative election, concluded that the only option before the Convention lay between an appointment by Electors chosen by the people and an immediate appointment by the people. Nevertheless, neither of these alternatives could be carried through the Convention. On August 24, both were defeated: an immediate election by a vote of 9 states to 2, a mediate election by 6 to 5.

The Convention was now at a standstill. Article X, section 1, of the printed plan—the draft of a constitution reported August 6 by the Committee of Detail—dealt comprehensively with the location of executive power and with the institution, unity, style, title, appointment, term, and eligibility of the Executive; but it could not be brought to a vote. Some parts of it indeed were tentatively approved and others modified; but on August 24, the consideration of its last two clauses, relative to term and eligibility, was postponed. The effect of the postponement was to kill the whole section; for it was the practice of the Convention to divide complicated propositions, to vote separately on each part, and then to vote again upon the whole. No question was finally determined by a vote upon the part; only a vote upon the whole was conclusive.

That a chasm existed in this part of the constitution was made plain on August 31, when a direction to the national legislature—that they should, as soon as might be, after their first meeting, choose the President of the United States—was struck out of the printed plan on the ground that this point, of choosing the President, had not yet been finally determined. On the same day the whole problem was referred for report to a Grand Committee, a committee of a member from each state present.

This committee, appointed by ballot, was composed in its majority of men favorable to an election of the President by the people. At least six of its eleven members had declared a preference for this mode as against all others: Rufus King of Massachusetts, Gouverneur Morris of Pennsylvania, John Dickinson of Delaware, Daniel Carroll of Maryland, James Madison of Virginia, and Abraham Baldwin of Georgia. Of the remaining five, Hugh Williamson of North Carolina had argued against a popular election but had himself suggested, as a cure to the difficulty that troubled him, the device of plural voting. Pierce Butler of South Carolina was something of a state partisan, but he preferred an appointment by Electors chosen by the people to an appointment by the national legislature. Nicholas Gilman of New Hampshire was by inclination a follower of such men as Gouverneur Morris; his views on the electoral system are not reported. David Brearley of New Jersey greatly respected the opinions of William Paterson, and Paterson on July 19 had supported a suggestion by Rufus King that the President be appointed by Electors chosen by the people. Only Roger Sherman of Connecticut had shown himself unreservedly opposed to an absolute appointment of the President by the people; the event was to show that he would accept, by way of compromise, a system of popular nomination coupled, in certain contingencies, with an eventual election by the national legislature.

On September 4, the committee made its report. It was at once apparent that the mode of absolute election by the national legislature had been rejected; for it was recommended, nearly at the beginning, that the President should hold his office for four years and be indefinitely re-eligible, two propositions long recognized as inconsistent with a legislative election. The mode proposed was, however, very complex. Each state was to appoint, in such manner as its legislature might direct, a number of Electors equal to the whole number of Senators and members of the House of Representatives to which the State might be entitled in the national legislature. The Electors were to meet in their respective states and vote by ballot for two persons as President, one of whom at least should not be an inhabitant of the same state with themselves. They were to make a list of all the persons voted for and of the number of votes for each, which list they were to sign and certify and transmit sealed to the seat of the general government, directed to the President of the Senate. The President of the Senate was in that House to open all the certificates, and the votes were then and there to be counted. If it were found that a majority of the Electors had concentrated their suffrages on a single man, giving him more votes than anybody else, that man was to be the President. If a majority had given an equal vote to two—or three—persons, the Senate was to choose by ballot one of them for President. If no candidate were the choice of a majority, then from the five highest on the list the Senate was to choose by ballot the President. The national legislature was to have authority to determine the time of choosing and assembling the Electors and the manner of certifying and transmitting their votes.

Viewed in the large, this was the plan of popular election, as modified by its proponents to take care of the difficulties of Negro representation and state favoritism. It had been much altered, however, in detail.

Great concessions had been made to the smaller states. Pursuing the idea that the presidential Electors and those who appointed them might be actuated by local rather than national views, might consider themselves as agents for the interests of their particular states rather than as representatives of the whole, the committee had gone far beyond the proposals originally made to obviate this difficulty—the double vote for President and the requirement of a majority for an absolute choice. In the initial election the advantage enjoyed, from the superiority of numbers, by the large states was to be diminished by allowing to each state two electoral votes beyond the number to which its population entitled it. In the eventual election each state, regardless of size, was to be given an equal vote in choosing the President out of the five highest on the return. To explain these concessions we need not lose ourselves in metaphysical definitions of the public will. Madison, to be sure, tells us that "in our complex system of polity, the public will as a source of authority, may be the will of the people as composing one nation; or the will of the States in their distinct and independent capacities; or the federal will, as viewed, for example, through the Presidential electors, representing in a certain proportion, both the nation and the States." But there is no evidence and little probability that such considerations entered into the deliberations of the committee. Madison said all that needed to be said when he explained these provisions "as the result of a compromise between the larger and smaller States, giving to the latter the advantage in selecting a President from the candidates, in consideration of the advantage possessed by the former in selecting the candidates from the people."

Great concessions had also been made to the particularists in the Convention. In the choosing of Representatives, care had been taken to reserve the right of election to the people; the manner, indeed, in which the people should exercise this valuable right had not been precisely adjusted: Each state was left to fix it according to its own particular prejudices; but the national legislature had been given an original and concurrent power to make and alter the state regulations on this subject—a power which could be used to prevent abuses or to promote uniformity. In the choosing of Electors, no such care was exhibited. The right of appointment was not to be exclusively vested in the people but was to be given into the possession of the state legislatures to be imparted by them to whomsoever they might severally wish, or to be exercised directly. No power, either original or concurrent, was to be given to the national legislature that might enable it to control the disposition of this right of appointment.

Such was the plan of the Grand Committee, the Committee of Eleven. When it was brought to debate in the Convention, it was attacked mainly on a single ground: The Senate was an improper body to make the eventual election. A great many members were convinced that, for one reason or another, the Electors would seldom come to a definitive choice; they would make the candidates, but the Senate would make the President. Colonel Mason even estimated the odds: "Nineteen times out of twenty the President would be chosen by the Senate." And the powers of the Senate were such that it ought not to be entrusted with this duty. The Senate was not merely a branch of the national legislature. It had legislative powers of its own: With the President it could make treaties that were to be the laws of the land. It had judicial powers, for it was to be the Court of Impeachments. It had executive powers, for it was to advise and consent to all important appointments, even to those in the judiciary department. With all these powers, and the President in its interest (for an officer is the officer of those who appoint him), the Senate would depress the other branch of the legislature and aggrandize itself in proportion. As for the President, he "would not be the man of the people as he ought to be, but the Minion of the Senate."

As a consequence of these representations, the Convention,

upon a suggestion by Sherman, substituted the House of Representatives for the Senate as the body to make the eventual election. To maintain the equality of suffrage enjoyed by the several states in the Senate, the vote in the House was to be taken by states and not by heads, the representation from each state having one vote. To quiet the fears of those who thought that a very few states might make the President, they alone being present, a quorum for the purpose was made to consist of a member or members from two thirds of the states, and a majority of all the states was made necessary to a choice.

A few other amendments were made to the report of the committee. No person was to be appointed an Elector who was a member of the national legislature or who held an office of profit or trust under the United States. The number of votes required for a definitive choice by the Electoral College was to be a majority of the Electors appointed, rather than of those authorized to be appointed or of those who had actually cast their votes—a change of convenience, designed to facilitate the reaching of a decision in the event that some states should neglect to appoint Electors or that some Electors should neglect to attend the College. The sealed certificates transmitted by the Electors to the President of the Senate were to be opened by that officer, and the votes were to be counted, in the presence of the House of Representatives as well as in that of the Senate. The House of Representatives, when called upon to make the eventual election, was to ballot "immediately." The national legislature was empowered to determine the day upon which the Electors should give in their votes, as well as the time of their appointment and assembly—but this day was to be the same throughout the United States.

Agreement having been reached on every point, the plan

of constituting the Executive was referred, with the rest of the proceedings of the Convention, to a Committee of Style and Arrangement. The committee reported the Constitution on September 12. In the section directing the mode of electing the President it made no substantial change in the plan previously approved by the Convention—only a few verbal alterations. On September 17 the Constitution was agreed to by the unanimous consent of all the states present.

What did the framers of the Constitution intend by this complex mode of electing the President? Did they mean to exclude the people from all participation in the important choice? Were the Electors "to make the election according to their own will, without the slightest control from the body of the People"? It is the fashion nowadays, it has been the fashion for over a century, to return affirmative answers to these last two questions. The Founding Fathers would have answered them, indeed did answer them, otherwise. Madison, after the plan had been adopted by the Convention, had no hesitancy in saying that "the President is now to be elected by the people." In the Virginia ratifying convention, he explained over and over again that the President was to be "the choice of the people at large." In the First Congress he spoke of the President as being "appointed at present by the suffrages of three million people." Randolph, defending the plan in Virginia, declared categorically that "the electors must be elected by the people at large." Mason, though he denounced the popular election as an *ignis fatuus* on the ground that the President would not be chosen once in fifty times by the people, because a majority of votes was required, nevertheless took it for granted that the people would appoint the Electors. Hamilton in No. 68 of the *Federalist* repeatedly stated that the appointment of the President was to be referred in the first instance to an immediate act of the people of

America, to be exerted in the choice of persons for the temporary and sole purpose of making the appointment: "It was desirable that the sense of the people should operate in the choice of the person to whom so important a trust was to be confided. This end will be answered by committing the right of making it, not to any pre-established body, but to men, chosen by the people for the special purpose, and at the particular conjuncture." In No. 77 he again spoke of the Electors as "persons immediately chosen by the people." Wilson told the Pennsylvania ratifying convention that the choice of the President was brought as nearly home to the people as was practicable: "With the approbation of the state legislatures, the people may elect with only one remove." Charles Pinckney remarked in the Senate that "this important officer, this intended man of the People," was to look to the people "for applause or subsequent appointments." [1] Daniel Carroll and Rufus King went so far as to pronounce unconstitutional any mode of appointing the Electors other than by a vote of the people.[2] These men had all been members of the Federal Convention. Other politicians read the Constitution in the same way. Senator Samuel Smith of Maryland, for example, declared in 1803 that "the intention of the convention was that the election of the chief officers of the government should come as immediately from the people as was practicable." [3] Smith was a Republican. Senator Timothy Pickering of Massachusetts, a Federalist, "believed it to be the intention of the Constitution, that the people should elect." [4]

These quotations disprove the views of those who say that

---

[1] 10 *Annals of Congress*, 129, 142 (1800).

[2] 2 *Annals*, 1857 (1791); 29 *Annals*, 216, 223 (1816). Rufus King to Cyrus King, September 29, 1823 (*The Life and Correspondence of Rufus King*, C. R. King, ed. [New York, 1894-1900], VI, 532-534).

[3] 13 *Annals*, 88 (1803).

[4] 13 *Annals*, 123 (1803).

the framers of the Constitution distrusted the people and feared popular election. It is clear, on the contrary, that the framers wanted and expected the popular principle to operate in the election of the President. Still, these quotations do not prove that no other principle was recognized by the Constitution. The words of that instrument are as follows: "Each State shall appoint, in such manner as the legislature thereof may direct, a number of electors. . . ." In earlier times many ingenious arguments were made to prove that a discretionary power in the state legislatures to direct the mode of appointing Electors does not include a power of appointing them themselves. "It seems to me," said Representative John H. Bryan of North Carolina in 1826, "that the Constitution here, by the use of the word *State*, means the Commonwealth, the political society—the People, or at least that portion of them who exercise the elective franchise; and therefore, that whenever the State Legislatures have exercised the power of appointing the electors, instead of directing the mode in which the State should appoint them, they have violated the rights of the people." [5] Bryan was echoing the words of Daniel Carroll and Rufus King, but, for all that, his reasoning will not withstand analysis. Too many members of the Federal Convention expressed a contrary view. Elbridge Gerry in 1789 took it for granted that the President might be elected by Electors appointed by the state legislatures.[6] Baldwin in the same debate said that the President was "to be appointed by electors chosen by the people themselves or by the State Legislatures." [7] Madison upon at least two occasions—in No. 45 of the *Federalist* and in the House of Representatives on January 14, 1791—conceded that the Electors

[5] II *Register of Debates*, 1628 (1826).
[6] 1 *Annals*, 536 (1789).
[7] 1 *Annals*, 557 (1789).

might constitutionally be chosen by the state legislatures. An incident that occurred in the Federal Convention on June 21 removes every doubt. General Pinckney, who had already failed to secure an election of the House of Representatives by the several legislatures, moved "that the first branch, instead of being elected by the people, should be elected in such manner as the Legislature of each State should direct." Hamilton was quick to see the joker; he "considered the motion as intended manifestly to transfer the election from the people to the State Legislatures."

In the light of all the evidence it seems fair to say that the Founding Fathers meant to invite but not to compel a popular appointment of Electors. As for the Electors themselves, it is surely wrong to suppose that they were expected to act in complete independence of the persons who appointed them. Without asserting that they were meant to be the automata which they eventually became, mere agents without discretion, we must look upon them as a medium for ascertaining the public will. John Clopton of Virginia, speaking in 1803, correctly characterized them as follows: "The Electors are the organs who, acting from a certain and unquestioned knowledge of the choice of the people, by whom they themselves were appointed, and under immediate responsibility to them, select and announce those particular citizens [who bear the stamp of public confidence], and affix to them by their votes an evidence of the degree of public confidence which is bestowed upon them." [8]

[8] 13 *Annals*, 423 (1803).

2. The Twelfth Amendment

In the debates that intervened between the dissolution of the Federal Convention and the adoption of the proposed Constitution by the requisite number of states, few objections were made to that part of the system which related to the mode of electing the President. Governor Clinton of New York, writing as Cato in the *New York Journal*, denounced the use of intermediate Electors and the provision for transferring the election, in certain contingencies, to the House of Representatives: "It is a maxim in republics that the representative of the people should be of their immediate choice; but by the manner in which the president is chosen, he arrives to this office at the fourth or fifth hand, nor does the highest vote, in the way he is elected, determine the choice, for it is only necessary that he should be taken from the highest of five, who may have a plurality of votes." George Mason, in the Virginia ratifying convention, made similar strictures as to the contingent election. But the leading opponent of the Constitution, Richard Henry Lee, in the *Letters of a Federal Farmer*, thought the election of the Executive to be "properly secured." And Hamilton noted the general satisfaction in No. 68 of the *Federalist*: "The mode of appointment of the chief magistrate of the United States is almost the only part of the system, of any consequence, which has escaped without severe censure, or which has received the slightest mark of approbation from its opponents. The most plausible of these, who has appeared in print, has even deigned to admit that the election of the president is pretty well guarded. I venture somewhat further, and hesitate not to affirm, that if the manner of it be not perfect, it is at least excellent. It unites in an eminent degree all the advantages the union of which was to be wished for."

No part of the plan of appointment seemed less open to blame than that which required the presidential Electors to cast two votes for President, one of which at least must be for a man who was not an inhabitant of the same state with themselves. Taken in conjunction with the requirement of a majority for an absolute choice, this provision put it out of the power of any state, however large, by itself to choose a President from among its own inhabitants; it almost of necessity compelled the selection of a continental character. "The second best man in this case would probably be the first, in fact," Madison had remarked in the Federal Convention. Very probably he remembered how the Greek generals, called upon to decide who had performed the best service in the war against Xerxes, had yielded individually to Themistocles, though, out of envy, unwillingly: Delivering their suffrages at the altar to determine who was most worthy, every one gave the first vote for himself and the second for Themistocles.[1]

Nevertheless the double voting system was an almost immediate failure, and in 1804 it was abandoned. To under-

[1] The incident is recorded by Herodotus and Plutarch. In 1816 Senator Samuel W. Dana of Connecticut cited it in explanation of the double voting system (29 *Annals*, 222).

stand the reasons for its failure we must now notice the office of Vice President and the mode of choosing its incumbent.

In every government where the executive power is vested in one man, occasions must sometimes arise when the one man needs a substitute. The members of the Federal Convention were well aware of this fact. They had in their eye a long line of regency acts passed by the British Parliament to deal with royal illnesses, absences, and minorities. They knew what the states had done to take care of similar contingencies; indeed, they had had an object lesson in 1776, when the physical incapacity of Governor Henry had thrown an added burden on John Page, President of the Virginia Council of State. Now in Philadelphia they heard the advocates of a plural executive and a Council of State raise the question pointedly. "The Single Head may be Sick," said Benjamin Franklin. "Who is to conduct the Public Affairs in that Case? When he dies, who are to conduct till a new election?" George Mason professed himself equally puzzled: "If there is no Council of State, and the executive power be vested in a single Person; what are the Provisions for its proper Operation, upon casual Disability by sickness or otherwise?" "Vacancies also must happen," said Edmund Randolph. "How can these be filled?"

The Constitution gave remarkably clear answers to these questions. It provided a presidential substitute, and it left no doubt as to who that substitute is to be. The Vice President was made the man in whom, when occasion arises, the presidential authority is to be vested; no man can be put over him. Nor did the Constitution leave any doubt as to the nature and extent of the powers and duties belonging of right to a Vice President acting as President: He was to exercise the whole, not merely a portion, of the presidential authority—to discharge all, not merely some, of the presidential duties; simultaneously he was to be relieved of the only substantive duty assigned to him by the Constitution—the presidency of the Senate. In England, by contrast, anyone might be named regent, and his powers might be variously limited— arrangements that had been productive of much difficulty and discord.

In devising a mode for selecting the Vice President, the Founding Fathers, however, were confronted by a difficult problem. The term of the President was four years; if he were to die or become otherwise incapacitated soon after his election, the Vice President, chosen for the same term, might be called upon to exercise the office of President for a considerable period of time. Unless the country was to be exposed to all the evils of a weak and inefficient administration, it was imperative that the Vice President, equally with the President, should be of the highest respectability, integrity, and capacity, a man possessing and worthy of the confidence of the nation. But how could such a man be brought into such an office? Certainly he would not seek it. The vice presidency, as a member of Congress once remarked, is "a situation certainly not calculated to inspire or satisfy the expectations of an ambitious man." [2] John Adams declared it the most insignificant office that ever the invention of man contrived or his imagination conceived—almost the only one in the world in which patience and firmness are useless. [3] Madison thought it an unprofitable dignity. [4] Jefferson found it

[2] Thomas Lowndes of South Carolina (13 *Annals*, 709 [1803]).

[3] *Letters of John Adams addressed to his Wife*, C. F. Adams, ed. (Boston, 1841), II, 133. *The Works of John Adams*, C. F. Adams, ed. (Boston, 1850-1856), IX, 573.

[4] Madison to Jefferson, October 17, 1788; Madison to Washington, November 5, 1788 (*The Writings of James Madison*, G. Hunt, ed. [New York, 1901-1910], V, 270, 303).

the only office in the world about which he was unable to decide whether he would rather have it or not have it.[5] One might as readily expect a theatrical player of the first magnitude to seek the role of understudy to one of his rivals as a man of presidential caliber to seek the vice presidency.

Nor was it likely that the people, either directly or through Electors, would solicit such a man. As Senator Plumer once remarked: "In electing a *subordinate officer*, men do not, they will not, seek for, or require, those qualifications which they deem requisite for *supreme* command."[6] Calculating upon the durability of human life, the people, in their choice of Vice President, would be influenced by considerations by which they ought not to be governed. They would select some popular man for qualities other than those which would fit him for the station of President. They would say: He is a good man—he can preside with credit over the Senate. And they would forget that he might be called to the exercise of higher duties.

Such was the problem that the Founding Fathers, having created the office of Vice President, were called upon to solve. That it actually appeared to them in this light seems proved not merely by the mode of appointment which they adopted but by the mode which they rejected, for the Founding Fathers had a model which they might have followed. Some of the states had retained from colonial days the two offices of Governor and Lieutenant Governor, and in those states the people gave their votes for one candidate, by name, to be Governor and for another to be Lieutenant Governor. The practice was perfectly familiar to the members of the

[5] *The Works of Thomas Jefferson*, P. L. Ford, ed. (New York, 1904-1905), VIII, 262.

[6] William Plumer, *Memorandum of Proceedings in the United States Senate*, E. S. Brown, ed. (New York, 1923), p. 64.

Federal Convention. Why then did they not adopt it? Why did they not authorize the presidential Electors, after choosing the President by ballot, to choose the Vice President by separate ballot? In 1803 Senator Timothy Pickering offered a conjecture: "The Governors and Lieutenant Governors were chosen for one year. The inferiority of rank and importance attached to the office of Lieutenant Governor, would naturally induce the people to think a man competent to the duties of that office, although his qualifications should be decidedly inferior to those they would deem requisite in the man they would choose for their Governor; and no material inconvenience would be apprehended from the choice of such a Lieutenant Governor, because he would administer the Government for so short a period—a portion only of one year. But to administer the affairs of a great nation more circumspection was necessary, and a longer continuance in office. The President and Vice President were to be chosen for four years. In case the office of President became vacant, the Vice President would succeed and be charged with all the duties of the President; and this might happen to be for two or three years, or even for four years, if the President should die between the time of his election and the period of taking upon himself the Government. It was therefore of the highest importance to place the election of Vice President on such ground as, if possible, would necessarily produce the choice of one every way qualified for the office of President." [7]

The ground selected by the Founding Fathers was every way remarkable. To view it in proper perspective we must constantly bear in mind one negative fact. The presidential Electors were not allowed to choose a Vice President. They

[7] 13 *Annals*, 198 (1803).

had nothing to do with that officer, who, as far as they were concerned, might as well not have existed. They were confined, as Senator Uriah Tracy of Connecticut remarked, "to act with a single reference to the character and office of President, and were trusted with no power to give any opinion of the character or qualifications of a Vice President." [8] Hence it is that the original Constitution never notices an electoral vote for Vice President and contains no qualifications for the Vice President as such. The Vice President was voted for as President, and the requisite qualifications of age, citizenship, and residence were as President. [9]

Each Elector had two votes for President. In practice, he wrote the names of two persons, both constitutionally qualified to be President, on a piece of paper called a ballot, and put it in a box. He was not permitted to distinguish between them; he could not say, I want A for President and B for Vice President, or I want A for President but in a pinch I'll take B. Insofar as the Constitution was concerned he had cast two undiscriminating votes for President. Both of them would be counted. Either of them might make a President, but the Elector could not know which.

In the double vote, however, the Founding Fathers saw a chance to produce a worthy Vice President. If the man could not be brought to the office, perhaps the office could be imposed upon the man. And so they provided that "In every Case, after the Choice of the President, the Person having the greatest number of Votes of the Electors shall be the Vice President." Only if there should remain two or more who had equal votes was the Senate to choose from them by ballot the Vice President.

[8] 13 *Annals*, 170 (1803).
[9] Senator Tracy noted the fact (13 *Annals*, 170). So did Senator Plumer (*Memorandum*, p. 19). It has often been misunderstood.

It was not until the President was chosen that the Vice President came into view; and then he was noticed only to be announced. That is the key to the original plan. There were to be no candidates for Vice President and no contest for that office. Each Elector was to vote for two persons as President but for none as Vice President. The runner-up in the presidential election was automatically to become Vice President. Senator Tracy explained the system in a word: "[The second person] can have no existence until the first character is designated, and then seems to be discovered, not elected." [10]

The guiding principle of the system is plain. Two men, both worthy to be President, both possessed of the highest confidence of the people, were to be placed in condition to act as President in succession. Then if the President died, not only would the evils of vacancy be prevented but also a recurrence of choice more frequently than once in four years would be avoided. The whole problem of the presidential succession seemed solved by a mode of selection designed, not to secure a competent President of the Senate, but (in Boudinot's phrase) "to obtain the second best character in the union to fill the place of the first, in case it should be vacated by any unforeseen accident." [11]

On paper the plan seemed perfect. If it had worked—if each Elector, laying aside all attempts to give one of his two candidates for President an advantage over the other, had voted for two men, each possessing the qualifications requisite for that high office—it would then have been a matter of much indifference, with respect to the great interests of the nation, which became the President and which the Vice President. [12]

[10] 13 *Annals*, 170 (1803).
[11] Thomas Lloyd, *Congressional Register* (New York, 1789), II, 93.
[12] 13 *Annals*, 198 (Senator Timothy Pickering [1803]).

By putting it in the power of the minority Electors to choose which of the two majority candidates for President they preferred, the mode of election might even have been the means of checking and moderating the rage and violence of party spirit, and of controlling and putting down faction.[13]

But the plan of the Founding Fathers failed. The difficulty was that the Electors did not in fact vote for two equal men as President. They discriminated in their minds between the man they wanted for President and the man they wanted for Vice President. And the second man was often very inferior to the first. Consider, for example, the election of 1800. The Republicans, as the members of the anti-federalist or democratic party were then called, put up two men—Jefferson and Burr—and gave them equal votes in the Electoral College. Presumably, therefore, they would have been satisfied to see either of them put at the head of the government. But this was not the case. When the House of Representatives was called upon to break the tie, the Federalists exhibited a marked preference for Burr. And what happened? Did the Republicans permit Burr—their own candidate for President—to become President? They did not. They fulminated, stormed, and threatened civil war if the will of the people were thus to be defeated.[14] And the will of the people *would* have been

[13] 13 *Annals*, 536 (Representative Seth Hastings of Massachusetts [1803]).

[14] In 1803 Senator James Jackson reminded his auditors (Burr not among them) of the fact: "We are told that the candidates, on a former occasion, had an equal claim and equal pretensions to the office of President. He [Jackson] did not wish to make comparisons; but he could not but recollect that the attempt to supersede one of the candidates, and to place the other in his station, had endangered the Government; and . . . he believed it would not be questioned that, so far as concerned Georgia, it never was intended to give them an equal chance; and small and obscure as that little corner called Georgia is, had the measure been pursued to consummation,

defeated had Burr been chosen; for not one single Elector of either party had given him a bona fide vote as President. He had been put on the ticket "out of respect for the favor he had obtained with the republican party by his extraordinary exertions and successes in the New York election in [April] 1800." [15] But no one thought of him for the office of President. Jefferson had long distrusted him, and had habitually cautioned Madison against trusting him too much.[16] Monroe thought him an unfit character.[17] These were Virginians. But even in Burr's own state, Hamilton "could scarcely name a discreet man of either party" who did not think "Mr. Burr the most unfit man in the United States for the office of President." [18] Theodore Sedgwick remarked: "It is very evident that the Jacobins dislike Mr. Burr as President—that they dread his appointment more than even that of General Pinckney." [19]

Or take the election of 1796. The Federalist candidates were Adams and Thomas Pinckney—both nominally candidates for the presidency. But Pinckney was not in reality the

which had been attempted on that occasion, she would have flown to arms, and South Carolina would have joined her to do justice to the interest of the nation" (13 *Annals*, 158). Jackson had been Governor of Georgia in 1801.

[15] Jefferson, *Works*, I, 381. On the selection of Burr, see Henry Adams, *Life of Albert Gallatin* (Philadelphia, 1880), pp. 232-243.

[16] Jefferson, *Works*, I, 381.

[17] Monroe to Madison, October 9, 1792 (*The Writings of James Monroe*, S. M. Hamilton, ed. [New York, 1898-1902], I, 242-244).

[18] Hamilton to Bayard, December 27, 1800 (*The Works of Alexander Hamilton*, J. C. Hamilton, ed. [New York, 1851], VI, 500-501).

[19] Sedgwick to Hamilton, January 10, 1801 (Hamilton, *Works*, VI, 513). In 1796 Oliver Wolcott, Jr., reported a similar fact to his father: "The antis, however, do not expect that Co. Burr will succeed, and they secretly wish that Mr. Adams may be elected to his present station" (George Gibbs, *Memoirs of the Administrations of Washington and John Adams* [New York, 1846], I, 387).

Federalists' second choice for President; if Adams had been dead, or had refused to run, they would not have tried to make Pinckney President. They thought of him as an honest man, who could not be made the tool or dupe of faction,[20] and who might make an interest for Adams, or even a diversion, in the state of South Carolina.[21] But on the other hand they looked upon him as half a democrat; his particular acquaintances were people of whose political opinions they did not approve; [22] it was disagreeable to think of elevating a person to the chief magistracy who had recently been hackneyed and vulgarized as Mr. Pinckney must have been in Europe; [23] the election of Mr. Pinckney would be a partial triumph of the French and their traitorous American partisans.[24] According to Chauncey Goodrich: "The experiment would be hazardous to place the Executive in a character little known in New England, and without any pre-eminent feature of public character, in any part of the Union. More than hundreds, on the score of merit, have a preferable claim to Mr. Pinckney. I do not mean to depreciate his worth. I value it." [25]

Adams himself would rather have been beaten by Jefferson, his opponent, than by Pinckney, his alternate. So at least he said, shortly after his election: "It is a delicate thing for me to speak of the late election. To myself, personally, 'my election' might be a matter of indifference or rather of aver-

[20] Oliver Wolcott, Jr., to Oliver Wolcott, Sr., November 19, 1796 (Gibbs, *Administrations*, I, 397).

[21] Jonathan Dayton to Oliver Wolcott, Jr., September 15, 1796 (*ibid.*, I, 383).

[22] Wolcott, Sr., to Wolcott, Jr., December 12, 1796 (*ibid.*, I, 408).

[23] Wolcott, Jr., to Wolcott, Sr., November 27, 1796 (*ibid.*, I, 402).

[24] Wolcott, Sr., to Wolcott, Jr., December 12, 1796 (*ibid.*, I, 409).

[25] Chauncey Goodrich to Oliver Wolcott, Sr., December 17, 1796 (*ibid.*, I, 412).

FERNALD LIBRARY
COLBY-SAWYER COLLEGE
NEW LONDON, N.H. 03257

sion. Had Mr. Jay, or some others, been in question, it might have less mortified my vanity, and infinitely less alarmed my apprehension for the public. But to see such a character as Jefferson, and much more such an unknown being as Pinckney, brought over my head, and trampling on the bellies of hundreds of other men infinitely his superiors in talents, services, and reputation, filled me with apprehensions for the safety of us all. It demonstrated to me that, if the project succeeded, our Constitution could not have lasted four years. . . . That must be a sordid people, indeed, a people destitute of a sense of honor, equity, and character, that could submit to be governed, and see hundreds of its most meritorious public men governed, by a Pinckney, under an elective government. . . . I mean by this no disrespect to Mr. Pinckney. I believe him to be a worthy man. I speak only by comparison with others.[26]

In the elections of 1789 and 1792 no difficulty was experienced from the attempts of the Electors to discriminate between their candidates for President and Vice President. Then, as now, there were two great political parties, "regular, organized parties, extending from the northern to the southern extremity, and from the Atlantic to the western limits of the United States." But, divided in everything else, they were united in the choice of Washington. There was never any chance that the electoral votes for Adams or for Clinton could equal or surpass those for Washington; consequently, the Electors could have no reason for throwing votes away from their candidates for the minor office.

After 1796, however, it became plain that the introduction of the designating principle into the system of electing a

[26] John Adams to Henry Knox, March 30, 1797 (Adams, *Works*, VIII, 535).

President and Vice President had made that system unworkable; for it confronted the presidential Electors, especially of the majority party, with an insoluble problem. They had to dispose of their votes in such a way as not only to bring in their two candidates but to bring them in in the right order.

They could do one of three things. They could give their two candidates an equal or nearly equal vote: That would exclude the minority candidates from either office; but then the minority Electors, by voting for the person intended by the majority to be Vice President and not voting for the person intended by them to be President, might contravene the intention of the majority and place in the executive chair a person not designed by the majority for that office. In 1800 the Republicans adopted this course with almost disastrous results. Nor did it escape their notice that had a single Federalist Elector voted for Burr, Burr would automatically have become President and Jefferson Vice President.[27]

Second, the majority could give one of the two votes to which they were entitled exclusively to one candidate and throw away the other: That would secure the office of President to the individual whom they preferred; but it would give up the office of Vice President to the minority. In 1796 the Republican party cast a unanimous vote for Jefferson and

[27] 13 *Annals*, 171. That the Federalists considered voting for Burr is certain: "The question has been asked, whether, if the Federalists cannot carry their first points, they would not do well to turn the election from Jefferson to Burr" (Cabot to Hamilton, August 10, 1800 [H. C. Lodge, *Life and Letters of George Cabot* (Boston, 1877), p. 284]). "I recollect well," said Uriah Tracy in 1803, "that it was thought probable, when the electoral votes were given, that Mr. Burr would have a vote or two in some of the Eastern States. If he had received but one, he would have been by an electoral choice the Constitutional President" (13 *Annals*, 171).

scuttled Burr. Had they won the election, Jefferson would have been President and Adams Vice President.

Finally, the majority could support both their candidates, but unequally, giving the second a few less votes than the first: That would entail a double risk. For one thing, it would give the minority a greater chance of bringing in their own candidate, at least as Vice President; alternatively, it would enable the minority, by switching their second votes from their own vice presidential candidate to that of the majority, to repair any deficiency in that individual's vote and, indeed, to make him President. In 1796 the Federalists pursued this middle course. Anticipating that Pinckney might defeat Adams with the aid of Southern votes, they deprived him of 18 votes in New England alone and 2 in Maryland; accordingly, Jefferson, the presidential candidate of the Republicans, became Vice President in a Federalist administration. If the Federalists had carried Pennsylvania, the story would have been different; in that event "the southern faction would unanimously have voted for Pinckney" [28] and so made him President, with Adams Vice President—unless indeed the Federalists had abandoned Pinckney altogether.

These difficulties, made even worse by the machinations of intra-party factions, turned the minds of men to a reform of the electoral system. The Federalists were first in the field with a specific proposal. On January 7, 1797, William Smith of South Carolina remarked in the House of Representatives that great inconveniences might arise from the existing mode of election; gentlemen must be satisfied that it could not answer the end intended, namely, to carry into effect the real intention of the Electors. He proposed, therefore, that the Electors be directed by the Constitution to designate whom

[28] Goodrich to Oliver Wolcott, Sr., December 17, 1796 (Gibbs, *Administrations*, I, 413).

they meant to be President and whom Vice President.[29] A year later John Marshall of Kentucky proposed a similar amendment in the Senate, but made no attempt to explain or press it.[30] Presently George Cabot complained of the Federalist apathy with regard to the subject of electing the President and Vice President: "The defect of the constitution in this particular is so obvious, and the inconvenience and absurdity of it so much felt, that I should imagine a proposition to amend it could not fail of success. It is certain that in the late election we were in danger of seeing a French President instead of an American placed in the chair, when a majority of the electors were truly Americans, merely because each elector could not constitutionally determine the character of his own vote. If this article in the Constitution is not amended, we shall be exposed to great embarrassments at the next election, as we were at the last. . . ." [31]

After the election of 1800 the reform movement was taken up by the Republicans. Attempts were made in 1801 and in 1802 to pass a designating amendment, but these were successfully repelled by the Federalists, to whom the defect of the Constitution had ceased to be obvious and who no longer felt its inconvenience and absurdity. The reasons for this Federalist change of opinion were clearly explained by Cabot: "I confess I was once desirous of a change of the kind now contemplated, believing it an indispensable means of preserving the government in good hands, and the country from the fangs of France, but we failed. Our opponents now wish the same things for purposes they approve, but which we think dishonorable and ruinous. Shall we be so weak as

[29] 6 *Annals*, 1824.
[30] 7 *Annals*, 493; Jefferson, *Works*, VIII, 360, 361.
[31] Cabot to Pickering, December 14, 1798 (Lodge, *George Cabot*, p. 189).

to promote in this manner the views and perpetuate the power of those in whom we cannot confide?" [32]

In 1803, however, the Federalist opposition was overcome in both Houses of Congress. The elections of 1804 were approaching, and it was evident to everyone that the Federalists intended to demand the vice presidency as the price of permitting Jefferson to continue in office. By threatening to transpose the Republican candidates by their votes in the Electoral College, they hoped to compel the Republicans to scatter their second votes and so permit the election to the vice presidency of the Federalist candidate for President. In short, they would do what the Republicans had done in 1796. To prevent this plan became the great object of the Republicans. Accordingly, they again introduced into Congress an amendment to the Constitution abolishing the double vote for President and requiring the Electors to vote for a President and Vice President by specific designation.

That this amendment looked forward to the election of 1804 rather than, as is commonly supposed, backward to the election of 1800, seems proved by the debates in the Senate. John Quincy Adams, a Federalist, "considered it as intending to prevent a federal Vice President being chosen." [33] Pierce Butler, a dissident Republican, thought the same thing: "There are motives operating in this body, and promoting this amendment, which, though not prominent, are powerful; it is said, if you do not alter the Constitution, the people called Federalists will send a Vice President into that chair; and this, in truth, is the pivot upon which the whole turns." [34]

[32] Cabot to Pickering, January 10, 1804 (*ibid.*, p. 336).

[33] 13 *Annals*, 128.

[34] 13 *Annals*, 87. In 1796 Butler had walked out of a Republican caucus in Philadelphia, offended at the decision to run Jefferson and Burr (Adams, *Works*, III, 417).

Colonel William Cocke, a roaring democrat, avowed that "he was actuated by a strenuous wish to prevent a Federal Vice President being elected to that chair." [35] John Taylor, a Republican of the old school and the leading supporter of the amendment, put the matter in the clearest of lights: "It has been urged, sir, by the gentlemen in opposition, in a mode as if they supposed we wished to conceal or deny it, that one object of this amendment, is to bestow upon the majority a power to elect a vice president. Sir, I avow it to be so. This is one object of the amendment. . . . Did the constitution intend that any minor faction should elect a vice president? If not, then an amendment to prevent it accords with, and is preservative of the constitution." [36]

The Federalists were quick to see the flaw in Taylor's argument. The whole difficulty, said the Federalists, came from the failure of the Republicans to observe the Constitution. Under the present state of parties they were perfectly able to place two persons of their own opinions in the two great offices; the minority could not do it. True, the majority could not determine which would be first and which second. That was a privilege wisely reserved by the Constitution to the minority party as a protection to their rights. But the majority had sought to take away this privilege. By bringing forward as their second candidate for President a man whom they never intended for that office, they had attempted to grasp all the benefits of President and Vice President within themselves to the total exclusion of the minority. If they persisted in this course, they must run the risk of losing the

[35] 13 *Annals*, 98. Butler characterized Cocke as a gentleman "who, after making a speech of an hour, sits down and roars out, the question! the question!" (13 *Annals*, 203).

[36] William Duane, *Report of a Debate in the Senate of the United States* (Philadelphia, 1804), p. 131.

vice presidency; but surely the evil would work its own cure. After a few elections the Republicans would see a necessity of a strict adherence to the spirit of the Constitution; they would put up two bona fide candidates for the presidency and leave it to the Federalists to arrange the two great executive offices between them, convinced that the true interests of the people lay in such an equal choice. As for the proposed amendment, it was destructive, not preservative, of the existing Constitution. Senator James Hillhouse of Connecticut summed up the whole argument: "Your amendment proposes to persuade the people that there is only one man of correct politics in the United States. Your Constitution provides a remedy against this, and says you must bring forward two. If the majority will select two and bring them fairly forward, how is it possible for the minority to bring any forward with effect?" [37]

The Federalist rebuttals fell on deaf ears. The Republicans were determined that Jefferson should be elected President in 1804. As for the vice presidency they cared not who held it; they wished only to hawk it for votes—to give it to some man who, like George Clinton, could carry New York. Besides, experience had taught them that the Federalists, for all their talk, if in their place, would do the same thing. And so in due course the Twelfth Amendment to the Constitution was passed by Congress and proposed to the states. During the summer of 1804 ratification was completed—in plenty of time to take care of the fall elections.

The Twelfth Amendment completely altered the original mode of electing the President and Vice President. It was no longer to be "the great and solemn duty of Electors, upon all occasions, to give their votes for two men who shall be

[37] *Ibid.*, p. 136.

best qualified for the office of President . . . two men, in either of whom they are willing to confide the Executive power of the Government." [38] Henceforth they were to vote for one man as President and another man as Vice President, indicating their choices in distinct ballots. When the votes were counted, the man having the greatest number of votes for President was to be President, and the man having the greatest number of votes for Vice President was to be Vice President—provided that, in each case, the greatest number equaled a majority of the whole number of Electors appointed. If no candidate for President had a majority, the House of Representatives, voting by states, was to choose a President from the persons have the three highest numbers on the list. If no candidate for Vice President had a majority, the Senate, voting by heads, was to choose a Vice President from the persons having the two highest numbers on the list. The same qualifications were required of the Vice President as of the President—a necessary precaution since he was no longer to be voted for as President. And it was provided that "if the House of Representatives shall not choose a President whenever the right of choice shall devolve upon them, before the fourth day of March next following [the date of the President's taking office], then the Vice-President shall act as President, as in the case of the death or other constitutional disability of the President."

The requirement of a majority for the Vice President was a novelty introduced to meet the objections of those who feared that, under the new arrangements, a very inferior candidate might be chosen.

[38] 13 *Annals*, 752 (Roger Griswold).

3. The Variety of Method

The Twelfth Amendment got rid of the double voting system, but it left unrestricted and uncontrolled the power of the several state legislatures to fix the manner of appointing the presidential Electors. The nature and tendency of that power is nowadays not very well understood, for the state legislatures, acting, as we shall see, under a kind of moral coercion, have established by parallel laws a uniform mode of appointment and have long since ceased to exercise the faculty of change. But the faculty of change remains. If at any time a state legislature should see fit to "interpose" in the interests of a particular candidate for the presidency by changing the mode of appointing Electors, it could not be prevented from doing so.

No mode of appointment is barred to the states. This absence of limitation is very remarkable. The Constitution has prescribed that Representatives in Congress shall be chosen in each state by the persons entitled to vote for the most numerous branch of the state legislature, but nowhere has it fixed the qualifications of voters in the presidential election. A state legislature may permit those who vote for Representatives in Congress to vote for Electors also; or it may devolve the choice of Electors on a different class of

citizens. It may remove the election from the people altogether and vest the power of appointment in itself, in the
Governor and State Senate, in the State Senate alone, in
the State House of Representatives, in a designated committee
of both Houses.[1] Indeed—insofar as the Constitution is concerned—there is nothing to prevent it from vesting that power
"in a board of Bank directors—a turnpike corporation—or a
synagogue."[2] Having determined who shall appoint, it is
free to determine the mode of appointment. If the election
has been confided to the people, the legislature can permit
each voter to vote for one, some, or all of the Electors to
which the state is entitled; it can require him to vote openly
by voice or secretly by ballot; it can make the definitive appointment of an Elector depend upon the concurrence of a
plurality of the voters in his constituency, or it can require
an absolute majority, leaving the ultimate choice to be made,
if necessary, by the people in a second election or by some
other authority. If the Legislature has kept the election to
itself, it may make the appointments by joint or concurrent
resolutions of both Houses, or by nomination by one House
and election by the other. Any mode, whether suggested by
the sense of equity and fair play or by the ferocity of faction,
is permissible.

Nor are the state legislatures subject to control by Congress. Here too there is a remarkable difference between the
directions of the Constitution respecting the manner of choosing Representatives and those respecting the manner of
choosing Electors. Charles Pinckney of South Carolina, a
member of the Federal Convention, explained it very well

[1] II *Register of Debates*, 1866 (Representative Michael Hoffman
of New York [1826]).

[2] II *Register of Debates*, 1405 (Representative Henry R. Storrs of
New York [1826]).

in 1800: "With respect to the House of Representatives . . . a right is in the first instance given to the State Legislatures to establish regulations for their election, and in the same clause a right is given to Congress—not to the House of Representatives but to Congress—not only to make regulations on the same subject, but to alter such as the State Legislatures have made; giving to Congress, in fact, a paramount authority, whenever they please, to regulate the elections of the House of Representatives in any manner they think proper. Let us for a moment compare this with the directions of the Constitution respecting the Electors of a President. . . . By the Constitution, Electors of a President are to be chosen in the manner directed by the State Legislatures—this is all that is said. In case the State Legislatures refuse to make these directions there is no power to compel them; there is not a single word in the Constitution which can, by the most tortured construction, be extended to give Congress, or any branch or part of our Federal Government, a right to make or alter the State Legislatures' directions on this subject. The right to make these directions is complete and conclusive [and] subject to no control or revision." [3]

Such was the nature of the power in the beginning, and such it is now. An assertion made in 1892, that the power of each state legislature to determine for itself the manner of appointing Electors, had been abridged by the Fourteenth and Fifteenth Amendments to the Constitution, was dismissed by the Supreme Court with the comment that "from the formation of the government until now the practical construction of the clause has conceded plenary power to the state legislatures in the matter of the appointment of electors." [4] Nor has Congress ever sought to interfere with the ex-

[3] 10 *Annals*, 128-129.
[4] McPherson *v.* Blacker, 146 U.S. 35 (1892).

ercise of this power.[5] Indeed, for many years, it refused to fix a particular day for the choosing of Electors, lest it be made a question "whether the power of Congress extends to determining the manner of choosing, by virtue of possessing the power of determining the time of their being chosen." [6]

To enumerate the discordant and varying modes of election which prevailed in different states and at different times during the first few decades of the new government would serve no useful purpose. As a committee of the Senate once remarked, "It is a task alike impracticable and unprofitable; for they change with a suddenness which defies classification." [7] Some of them were very extraordinary. In 1792, for example, the North Carolina legislature divided the state into four districts and gave the appointment of three Electors for each district to the members of the state legislature resident therein.[8] In 1796 and 1800 the Tennessee legislature prescribed an even more exotic mode. In order "that the said electors may be elected with as little trouble to the citizens as possible," the state was divided into three districts and the

[5] Fitzgerald *v.* Green, 134 U.S. 377 [1890].

[6] 2 *Annals*, 1868 (1791). The fixing of a day would have tended to force a popular election in those states whose legislatures were not in session on the day fixed. So, at least, it was thought. In 1845 Congress overcame its scruples and fixed the Tuesday after the first Monday in November as the day for choosing Electors; this was nearly three weeks earlier than the day appointed by the constitution of South Carolina for the assembling of its legislature. To preserve the legislative mode of election, the Governor of this state, in every fourth year, called the legislature into extraordinary session in advance of the regular period.

[7] II *Register of Debates*, Appendix, p. 121. A table showing the methods of appointing electors, 1788-1836, is to be found in C. O. Paullin, *Atlas of the Historical Geography of the United States* (Washington and New York, 1832), p. 89. But this table does not, and could not, descend into detail.

[8] *Laws of North Carolina*, 1792, Chap. XV.

appointment of one Elector for each district was given to certain designated individuals resident therein—thirty-three persons in all.[9]

Three modes were usual: election by the legislature; election by the people in districts; election by the people on a general ticket. But each of these was susceptible of numerous variations.

In 1819 Senator Dickerson of New Jersey stated that "when the Legislatures have taken this power into their own hands, they have made the appointments sometimes by a joint vote of the two Houses, sometimes by concurrent vote, sometimes by compromise; sometimes the resolutions, under which the appointments have been made, have received the approbation of the Executive, when such approbation was necessary, and sometimes not." [10] In New York, under a law passed at a very early period and not repealed until 1825, each House, by majority vote, nominated a full slate of Electors; then the two Houses met in joint convention and, again by majority vote, reconciled their differences.

The district mode was even more variable. Sometimes the people voted in equal districts, each district choosing one Elector; but sometimes they voted in unequal and irregular districts, some large and some small, some to choose one Elector, some two, some three, and some four. Sometimes the election was by district pluralities and sometimes by district majorities. In 1792, to give an extreme illustration, Massachusetts was divided by its legislature into four districts, two of which were to vote for five Electors each, and two for three Electors each. A majority of votes was necessary for a choice; if a district failed to give a majority to its full complement of Electors, the legislature was to supply the de-

[9] *Laws of Tennessee* (Knoxville, 1803), pp. 109-111, 211-213.
[10] 33 *Annals*, 143.

ficiency from the candidates standing highest on the list, the number of candidates being limited to twice the number of places to be filled. As things turned out in 1792, the people, in their districts, chose five Electors and the legislature chose eleven.

Even the general ticket system, under which every voter voted for every Elector to which the state was entitled, was not uniform. Here too the plurality system competed with the majority system. Under the former, the persons having the greatest numbers of votes on the list of those voted for as Electors were declared appointed. Under the latter, no one could be appointed at the first trial unless he had received the votes of a majority of the persons voting; in case of a failure to elect, the legislature or the people, in a run-off election, filled the vacancies; in the second election the number of candidates was twice the number of places to be filled, and the candidates themselves were the persons having the greatest number of votes (but not a majority) at the first election. In New Hampshire, for example, no one was definitively elected by the people in the election of 1788; the legislature accordingly, in January, 1789, appointed five Electors from the ten persons who had received the greatest number of popular votes.

Viewed as a whole, the system of voting for Electors prior to the election of 1836 was multiform and unsteady. "Different rules prevail in the same State at different times, and in the different States at the same time, all liable to be changed according to the varying views and fluctuating fortunes of political parties." Such was the observation of an acute observer in 1826.[11] In the election of 1824, for example, twelve states voted by general ticket, six by the legislature, four

[11] II *Register of Debates*, 1367 (George McDuffie of South Carolina).

by districts, and two by a compound of districts and general ticket.[12] Of all the states Massachusetts was the most inconstant; not until 1828 did it appoint its Electors by the same mode twice in succession.

The evils of this system, or lack of system, were very apparent to the politicians who suffered from them. In every election the distribution of electoral votes among the several candidates for President was determined almost as much by the mode of election as by the sense of the people. In 1812, for example, a legislative choice in New Hampshire would have given the 8 votes of that state to Madison; the general ticket system gave them to De Witt Clinton.[13] Conversely, in the same year, the general ticket system in New Jersey would have given the 8 votes of that state to Madison; a legislative choice gave them to Clinton. In 1824 the general ticket system would have given Adams the entire vote of Maryland; under the district system, by a curious combination of circumstances, he obtained but 3 of its 11 votes. In the same year, under the district system, Crawford would have got 7 or 8 of North Carolina's 15 votes; under the general ticket system, faced by a coalition ticket manufactured by the supporters of Adams and Jackson, he got none. But illustrations make the point no clearer. It is self-evident that in any state where there are sectional divisions of opinion a vote by districts will produce a different result from a vote at large. It is also self-evident that a legislative election will produce a different result from a popular election if the majority of the legislature do not see eye to eye with a majority of the people.

[12] II *Register of Debates*, 1468 (Romulus M. Saunders of North Carolina).

[13] II *Register of Debates*, 1832 (Thomas Whipple, Jr., of New Hampshire).

It was bad enough that the states differed from one another; it was worse that they were inconsistent with themselves. "If the discordant systems adopted by the different States were to be permanent, it would afford some security for fair elections. But, so far from this, they are the subject of constant fluctuation and change—of frequent, hasty, and rash, experiment—established, altered, abolished, re-established, according to the dictates of the interest, the ambition, the whim, or caprice, of party and faction." [14] Such was the observation of a United States Senator in 1818. Representative Israel Pickens of North Carolina, two years earlier, denounced "the ridiculous and disgusting occurrences which ever have, and ever will attend this unsettled course," as "tending to degrade our representative government in the eyes of the world, and to lower it in our own estimation." [15] Representative Benjamin Huger of South Carolina in the same year took the same view. "Who indeed," he asked, "was not apprized of the various turns, and twists, and quirks, which had alternately been adopted by different States, or rather predominant factions in different States, to insure a result of the election of the day favorable to their wishes and views? How many and how frequent changes had been made in the mode of election, on the spur of the occasion, and to effect some temporary and factious purpose?" [16]

A few illustrations will give point to these remarks. In 1800 the two Houses of the Pennsylvania legislature were in collision. Thirteen of the twenty-five Senators were Federalists; however, a very large majority of the Assembly were Republicans, and the Assembly, having been recently elected, afforded a very fair representation of the relative strength

[14] 31 *Annals*, 180 (Mahlon Dickerson of New Jersey).
[15] 30 *Annals*, 303 (1816).
[16] 30 *Annals*, 340.

of the parties throughout the state. In the three previous elections Pennsylvania had voted by general ticket, but the law fixing this mode had expired by its own limitation. In this situation the Federalist members of the Senate, the "Federal Thirteen" or the "Spartan Band," as they were pleased to call themselves, determined to prevent the appointment of any Electors: If Pennsylvania would not vote Federalist, she would not vote at all. In this measure they persisted, in defiance of public opinion, until they forced a disgraceful compromise by which one half of the Electors were to be of one party and the other half of the other, except the odd one, who was given to the Assembly.

In 1812 a much bolder step was taken by the legislature of New Jersey. Not content with silencing the voice of the people, they determined to make them speak a language the very reverse of their wishes. How this was managed was explained a few years later by a Senator from that state: "In the year 1812, by a strange concurrence of circumstances, not necessary to be here detailed, a small majority of the legislature were in direct opposition to a very large majority of the citizens of the State. By a law which had been many years in existence, the Electors, as well as the Representatives in Congress, were to be elected by the people in a general ticket; the election was to take place early in November. The Legislature met late in October, and only eight days previously to the day of election; under the provisions of the law, nominations had been made for Electors and Representatives in Congress in all the counties of the State. Copies of these nominations had been transmitted to the Executive of the State, from which a general nomination was made out, and transmitted by the Executive to all the county clerks, who had transmitted copies of the same to all the town clerks, by whom they had been duly advertised; all this had been done at considerable expense and trouble previously to the meeting of the Legislature. It will scarcely be believed that any Legislature would, under such circumstances, venture to arrest the progress of an election so far advanced and so near a completion. The legislature, however, repealed the election law, and took into their own hands the appointment of Electors. Expresses were sent into the different parts of the State, to give notice of this repeal, but not in time, for the citizens in many towns met and gave their votes for Electors and Representatives without knowing of the repeal of the law. The Legislature appointed eight Electors, not one of whom would have been appointed by the people under the late election law; and this the Legislature well knew; otherwise they would not have taken from the people the right of choosing Electors under the law. By this rash measure, which the people took care to reprobate at the next election, the majority in the State not only lost their vote, but were made to speak a language, as I before observed, the very reverse of their wishes." [17]

In 1824 the "Immortal Seventeen" in the New York Senate followed the example of the "Spartan Band" in Pennsylvania in 1800. These seventeen were the friends of William H. Crawford, candidate of the old Virginia Republicans for the presidency. If Crawford was to win the election, it was absolutely necessary that he have the 36 votes of New York. His best, indeed his only, chance of obtaining them was by a legislative appointment of the Electors; but the state elections of 1823 had turned on the question of electoral reform, and these elections had been won by the advocates of a popular appointment. In January, 1824, by the great ma-

[17] 31 *Annals*, 182-183 (Mahlon Dickerson [1818]).

jority of 110 to 5, the Assembly had passed a bill providing for the appointment of the Electors by the people. In these circumstances the Senate, "under the influence of infatuated and desperate party councils, shamelessly bid defiance to the known public will, and dared to try their strength against the mighty indignation of an insulted people." [18] By a vote of 17 to 13 they defeated the electoral bill. In August, at a special session called by the Governor to reconsider the subject of the electoral law, they interposed again, this time by refusing to act upon a bill passed by the Assembly. In the end they had their way; the New York Electors were appointed as usual by the legislature. But the fruits of victory were lost. A great revulsion of feeling swept through the state. At the fall elections those of the "Immortal Seventeen" whose terms were about to expire, succumbed to the popular vengeance; only one of them indeed ventured to stand for re-election, and he was defeated. Everywhere the opponents of the old Republican party prevailed. The election results were received at a time when the legislature was in session for the sole purpose of appointing presidential Electors. The Senate, thanks to the "Immortal Seventeen," held firm and nominated a Crawford-Clay coalition ticket; but the Assembly, under the influence of panic, nominated an Adams-Clay ticket and, in joint convention, carried it through the legislature. On the first ballot thirty-two of the thirty-six Electors on this ticket were appointed; but so close was the contest that on the second ballot the remaining four, all of them Clay Electors, were lost. [19]

[18] II *Register of Debates*, 1401 (Representative Henry R. Storrs of New York [1826]).

[19] The loss was occasioned by blank votes cast by the Adams men for these four places. Van Buren believed that they were intentionally lost "from a desire on the part of the Adams men to exclude Mr.

Incidents of this kind, repeated at almost every election, turned the minds of statesmen to reform. The power of the state legislatures to direct the manner of appointing presidential Electors was reprobated as "a rotten, a gangrenous part of our Constitution, which if not removed will infect and poison the body politic." [20] Uniformity was pronounced desirable. "The officer to be elected was the officer of the whole community, as much of Massachusetts as of Georgia, of Connecticut as of Kentucky. Why then should a different mode of election prevail in different States?" [21] And uniformity, it was said, was attainable only by a constitutional provision. As long as the mode of election was left to the various and varying counsels of the several states, such changes would be made by the prevailing parties as might answer their particular views. Experience had proved this. There had been exhibited between states, and parties in states, almost every four years, what might be called a political farce, but for the importance of the actors and the weight of the results.[22] No alteration made by any one state would produce a material change in the various modes existing throughout the

Clay from the House" (*Autobiography of Martin Van Buren*, J. C. Fitzpatrick, ed. [Washington, 1920], p. 145). Jabez D. Hammond was of the same opinion: "Did the Adams men, in the New York Legislature, act with good faith towards their Clay friends?" (Jabez D. Hammond, *The History of Political Parties in the State of New York* [Albany, 1841], II, 177). Whatever answer may be returned to this question, it is certain that the four electoral votes taken from Clay and given to Crawford brought Crawford's name instead of Clay's into the House of Representatives in 1825. Had the event been otherwise, Clay rather than Adams might have been President.

[20] 20 *Annals*, 310 (Representative Jabez D. Hammond of New York [1816]).

[21] 29 *Annals*, 224 (Senator Eligius Fromentin of Louisiana [1816]).

[22] 30 *Annals*, 302 (Representative Israel Pickens of North Carolina [1816]).

Union. It remained for the people, by an amendment to the Constitution, to remove the evil.[23]

Two courses were open to the people. They might give to Congress the power to prescribe a uniform mode of appointing Electors, or they might themselves prescribe such a mode. To the first course, however, there were many objections. It was extremely doubtful that Congress would exercise such a power, even if granted. It already had the power to regulate the election of Representatives, and the need for regulation was patent, for Representatives were chosen by a variety of modes as pernicious in its effect as that which governed the choice of Electors; but Congress had never yet ventured to touch the subject, so extremely delicate was it viewed. Indeed, it was said, Congress should never be allowed to touch it, except to make such regulations as should be perpetual. A power to prescribe a uniform mode is a power to change from one uniform mode to another. Might not the dominant party in Congress, in election after election, maintain itself in power, by shifting backwards and forwards from a uniform district system to a uniform general ticket system when the one or the other would produce results favorable to itself? "The consequence," said a leading reformer, "of allowing this body to be changing the mode of exercising this fundamental right, would be viewed by some of the States with great jealousy, particularly where it might be construed as done with the view of gaining some unfair political advantage; and it might often happen that the jealousy would be too well founded." [24]

A committee of the House of Representatives even went so

[23] Message of Governor Joseph C. Yates to the New York Legislature, January, 1924 (*State of New York, Messages from the Governors*, C. Z. Lincoln, ed. [Albany, 1909], III, 30).

[24] 30 *Annals*, 302 (Israel Pickens).

far as to suggest that Congress, if given the same power over the appointment of Electors as it actually had over the election of Representatives, might prescribe a non-uniform mode, so arranged by the party in power that a small minority of the people would elect a majority of the national Representatives and presidential Electors: "The mode of operation would be various, according to varying circumstances. Sometimes the object would be accomplished by changing the district into the general-ticket system; sometimes by an artificial arrangement of districts; and sometimes by a skilful combination of both. As nothing is too desperate for a faction, struggling for existence, let us suppose that they should prescribe, as they would have the unquestionable power to prescribe, that, in all those States where a majority of the people were favorable to their purposes the representatives [and electors] should be elected by a general ticket, thus suppressing the voice of the minority; and, that all the States opposed to their domination, should be divided into districts, in such manner that the minority of the people should elect a majority of representatives [and electors]. As examples of such high-handed proceedings are already to be found in the history of several of the State governments, the supposition that the General Government, with more powerful inducements to mislead it, will, at some future period, pursue a similar course, cannot be considered extravagant or improbable." [25]

Influenced by considerations such as these, the great body of reformers took the position that steadiness and uniformity in the mode of electing the President should be secured by the Constitution itself. Nor, it soon became clear, were they in any doubt as to what that mode should be. Four plans were

[25] 41 *Annals*, 853 (1823).

brought to debate. Perhaps the simplest was that proposed by Senator Abner Lacock of Pennsylvania in March, 1816: Let the President be chosen by a direct vote of the people in a nation-wide plebiscite—the people being defined as the persons in each state qualified to vote for the most numerous branch of the state legislature. If the intermediate Electors and electoral votes were dispensed with and the people were to give in their votes as they did in several states for their Governors, these votes to be returned to the state Executives and by them to the general government, there would be no occasion for the machinery of Electoral Colleges and, of course, no difficulty in fixing a uniform mode of election.[26] But Lacock's plan, like the similar one proposed in the Federal Convention, was regarded as wholly impracticable. Senator Jeremiah Mason of New Hampshire remarked that the qualifications of voters in the different states were so entirely different that the whole election would be unequal in its bearing on the different states: "One State has not, in some instances, according to its population, one-fourth of the votes which another State may give, etc. If there were no other objection to this new proposition, this would of itself be conclusive." [27]

A second plan was to extend the mode of legislative election from the states which practiced it to the rest of the Union; but as this mode was disliked by the people at large, it commanded no support.[28]

---

[26] 29 *Annals*, 220.

[27] 29 *Annals*, 223.

[28] In 1814 Representative William H. Murfree of North Carolina spoke in favor of such a plan (26 *Annals*, 856). It is a curious illustration of the influence of faction on principle that when, in 1800, Judge Jedediah Peck introduced a district bill in the New York Assembly, the Federalists opposed it as unconstitutional on the ground that the words "each state" imply that the state must act as a body

A third plan was to give the election to the people, voting uniformly in the several states by general ticket; but this system, too, was unpopular. In 1826 Representative George McDuffie, a leading advocate of reform, declared himself satisfied, by his own observation, that the people in all the states that had tried the general ticket system were opposed to it: "It is certain," he concluded, "that the People will never consent to the establishment of an uniform general ticket system, by an amendment to the Constitution." [29] His assertions were probably correct. In the previous year the people of New York, in a referendum, had exhibited a marked preference for the district system over any kind of general ticket system. [30]

The fourth plan was to establish a uniform mode of popular voting by districts. Let each state be divided by its legislature into a number of districts equal to the number of electoral votes to which it was entitled; let these districts consist of compact and contiguous territory and contain, as nearly as might be, equal numbers of persons; let the qualified voters in each district cast, either directly or through the agency of an intermediate Elector, one electoral vote for President. Such was the district system in its purest form. Sometimes the scheme was modified in such a way as to distinguish between the electoral votes allocated to a state on the basis of population and those allocated to it on the principle of state equality; in the so-called New Jersey plan, for example, two votes in each state were to be cast by the people at large and the rest by the people in districts.

This fourth plan, in one or another of its modifications, was

corporate and that, therefore, the Electors cannot be appointed by the people. The bill was rejected by a vote of 55 to 47.

[29] II *Register of Debates*, 1373.

[30] II *Register of Debates*, 1879 (Michael Hoffman of New York).

that which most of the reformers favored. It was repeatedly advocated by the leading statesmen of both parties—by Hamilton, Jefferson, Madison, Gallatin, Bayard, King, Macon, J. Q. Adams, Jackson, Van Buren, Hayne, Webster, and many others. It was approved, as Macon rightly said, by almost all the states.[31] The Virginia legislature, with extraordinary unanimity, upon several occasions, proposed to engraft the district system into the federal Constitution.[32] In 1816, when the same proposition was recommended to the several states by the legislature of North Carolina, it was adopted by the legislatures of a large majority of the states, and by those of two of the largest, New York and Virginia, almost unanimously.[33] The Senate of the United States more than once adopted, by the constitutional majority of two thirds, resolutions in favor of the district system; and in 1820 the House of Representatives sanctioned it by a vote of 92 to 54, wanting but a few votes of a constitutional majority.

But although everyone knew what to do, nothing was done. The reasons for non-action were purely political. The district system would have compelled the predominant party in every state to come into the contest fairly. As Rufus King remarked, it would have put all the people in the country on the same footing; the people in each district would have cast their vote for President according to a sense of their own interest, and a majority of districts, in a nation-wide constituency, would have chosen the President.[34] On the other hand, the existing arrangements permitted the predominant party in each state to rig each election in its own favor. By requiring the Electors to be appointed by the

[31] 41 *Annals*, 400 (1824).
[32] II *Register of Debates*, 1906 (John S. Barbour of Virginia).
[33] II *Register of Debates*, 1368, 1939 (George McDuffie).
[34] 29 *Annals*, 216 (1816).

legislature or by general ticket not only could the party suppress the votes of sections of the state opposed to it but it could also count those votes as if they had been cast for itself. Since victory, not equity, is the ordinary goal of politicians, since a great majority is preferable to a small one, the district system was much misliked by the practical politicians who controlled each separate state.

Nor was this all. Under the district system, the people of the United States would have been in fact what they are in theory, the fountain of political power. Under the alternative systems, political power flowed, not from the people, but from the leading politicians in the several states. If the appointment of Electors was by the legislature, the leaders of the majority party directly substituted themselves for the whole body of the state, the political interests of which might be very diverse. If the appointment was by general ticket, political power was virtually removed still more remotely from the people. A general ticket had, of necessity, to be formed by a caucus of the state legislature or by some other collection of individuals; a voter had no alternative at the polls but to decline his right to vote with possibility of effect or to give his aid to one or the other of the politically manufactured tickets. As between two systems, one of which reduced, the other of which increased, the weight and consequence of party politicians, it is not unnatural that the politicians at least should have preferred the general ticket system.

Throughout the Union, therefore, the question of reform tended to be debated on grounds of state power rather than national principle. The prevailing party in each state was generally the advocate for giving a united suffrage, regardless of the sentiments of divisions; the minority contended for allowing to every section its proper and distinct weight; and this, as a member of Congress remarked, was the general character of the majority and minority, no matter of what political complexion.[35] The presidential election of 1812 presented an instance of this rule that greatly impressed the minds of contemporary statesmen. "In Massachusetts no other mode could be tolerated by the Democratic part of the Legislature, but the choice by the people in districts; while in North Carolina it was claimed to be Republican to appoint by the Legislature. And, vice versa, the same political party that in North Carolina advocated the choice in districts, in Massachusetts was found to prefer either a Legislative choice or a general ticket." [36]

The struggle between the contending parties to render the mode of appointment in the several states subservient to their immediate views had an important effect on the reform movement; for it produced a conflict in the minds of the people, and of the reformers themselves, in which correctness and expediency were arrayed against each other. "All agree," said Jefferson in 1800, "that an election by districts would be best, if it could be general; but while 10 states choose either by their legislatures or by general ticket, it is folly and worse than folly for the other 6 not to do it." [37] "Is there a shadow of equity," asked another reformer, "in giving one State the advantage of a consolidated vote, while another is divided into districts and probably neutralized?" [38] Absolute justice required the establishment of a uniform district system throughout the Union; retributive justice compelled the establishment of a consolidated voting system in each state separately. And so it came about that the very men who most strenuously

[35] 30 *Annals*, 302-303 (Israel Pickens of North Carolina [1816]).

[36] 26 *Annals*, 838 (William Gaston of North Carolina [1814]).

[37] Jefferson to Monroe, January 12, 1800 (Jefferson, *Works*, IX, 90).

[38] 41 *Annals*, 1072 (George McDuffie [1824]).

advocated the district system for the nation were often the principal architects of the general ticket system in their own states. Madison, for example, never ceased to extol the merits of a uniform district system, but in Virginia in 1800 he supported the replacement of the district system by the general ticket system. His reasons were apparent: In 1796 the electoral district dominated by Loudoun County had cast a Federalist vote for President; the general ticket system would enable the Republicans to seize this vote and count it for Jefferson in 1801. Other politicians in other states pursued a similar course, and justified it by pointing at each other. No one could doubt the correctness of their logic. Granted that some states appointed their Electors in a block, what real choice had the others? They had only an option between falling into the same system or submitting to a material diminution of their net weight in the election. Those who in one breath advocated the establishment of a uniform mode of voting by districts, and in the next proposed the abolition of the district system in their own state, cannot rightly be charged with inconsistency. Nevertheless, the effect of the contrast between the habitual language of reform and the habitual practice of reformers was very deleterious.

More important, however, was the disappearance in the course of these partisan struggles of one of the chief motives of constitutional change. The great good to be obtained from an amendment to the Constitution was steadiness and uniformity in the mode of appointing Electors; the great evil to be avoided was variety and change. But, as time went on, a single, unvarying mode came to be adopted in all the states separately. This was the general ticket system. No other system could stand up to it.

The district system was the first to go. Sometimes it fell a victim to the general ticket, sometimes to the legislative mode. Virginia was the first to abandon it; Maryland was the last. The reasons for its abandonment, we have already given; but let us repeat them in the prophetic words of a Senate committee: "If uniformity by districts is not established by the free consent of the States, uniformity by general ticket or legislative ballot, must be imposed by necessity. For, when the large States consolidate their votes to overwhelm the small ones, those, in their turn, must concentrate their own strength to resist them. A few States may persevere, for some time, in what they believe to be the fairest system; but, when they see the unity of action which others derive from the general ticket and legislative modes of election, they will not, and, with due regard to their own safety, they *cannot*, resist the temptation of following the same plan." [39] These words were written in 1826; ten years later the district system had vanished from the scene.

The legislative mode was stronger than the district system but weaker than the general ticket. Attacked from the beginning as unconstitutional, even by members of the Federal Convention, the legislative mode grew increasingly unpopular. Most of the "ridiculous and disgusting occurrences" cited by reformers were connected with it. We have observed the actions of the "Spartan Band" and the "Immortal Seventeen" in Pennsylvania and New York, respectively; in 1808, in 1812, and in 1816, the legislature of Massachusetts had acted with a similar disregard of the general will. We have seen also how, in one election, the New Jersey legislature gave to its Electoral College its own political image in defiance of the known will of the people.

Of all modes, the legislative was the most obviously corrupt. "When met in the Legislature, innumerable are the oppor-

[39] II *Register of Debates*, Appendix, p. 127. Senator Thomas Hart Benton of Missouri was the author of this report.

tunities and temptations to barter votes. Judges, generals, governors, and many other State officers are to be elected. Towns are to be laid off, peradventure on some member's land. New counties are to be erected for the benefit of a clerk, a sheriff, and a colonel; peradventure, also, members at the time. Many other local interests are to be accommodated. The members interested in all these domestic questions, are laid under violent temptations to exchange votes with the friends of a Presidential candidate." [40] Such were the general observations of a consummate politician in 1824; they have all the signs of a factual relation.

The eventual disappearance of this mode was foreshadowed by an incident which occurred in North Carolina in 1812. This state for many years had chosen its Electors by single-member districts. Its sentiments had always been predominantly Republican, but in 1812 it seemed likely that the Federalists might gain the votes of many districts. The country was engaged in a struggle with England; combinations were the order of the day; and the Federalist slogans were a speedy peace and a glorious termination of the war. The votes of Pennsylvania and North Carolina were necessary to secure the re-election of Mr. Madison; if the former were lost, the latter must stand firm. In these circumstances the legislature in North Carolina interposed. It abolished the district system, and "to make assurance doubly sure" it transferred the appointment of Electors to itself rather than to the people voting by general ticket. In justification of this action it explained that the true sense of the people could not be ascertained at a time when ten thousand of the independent freemen of North Carolina were abroad fighting the battles of their country; a legislative appointment would secure to

[40] 41 *Annals*, 175 (Thomas Hart Benton).

Mr. Madison 15 Republican votes; a popular appointment, that is to say, an appointment by the people who remained at home, might give these votes to De Witt Clinton. The explanation was not accepted by the people; and the consequences were instructive. Representative Romulus Saunders of North Carolina related them to his colleagues some years later: "The vote was in conformity, no doubt, with the wishes of a large majority of the State; yet the People, who had before been somewhat indifferent to this election, were roused from their apathy at what they considered so daring an usurpation of their elective franchise—the whole State was thrown into the most violent commotion, and this act was well nigh changing the power of the two great political parties of the State. So that, before the next Presidential election, the dominant party was compelled to compromise between the district system, and the appointment by the Legislature, and adopt the general ticket. Thus has stood the thing since: the People have acquiesced, not through choice, but because they have been taught to believe it was necessary for the preservation of the relative influence of the State." [41]

By 1836 the era of change was over. In the election of that year and in every election up till the Civil War, the choice of Electors was by general ticket in every state except South Carolina, where it was by the legislature.[42] After the Civil

[41] II *Register of Debates*, 1468.

[42] In South Carolina the parish system and the representation of property in the state legislature permitted the low country to govern the up country, the minority to govern the majority. The general ticket system would have transferred the appointment of Electors from the "saints" of the parishes to the "real men" of the state; it was therefore opposed by the former as contrary to sound principle and the compromise of 1808. See the debates of the General Assembly in December, 1855 (*South Carolina Legislative Times*, pp. 78, 84, 99, 131).

War South Carolina also adopted the general ticket system, and, with three exceptions, no other system has been used by any state from that time to this. Florida in 1868 chose its Electors by a viva voce vote of its legislature; [43] Colorado in 1876 also chose by the legislative mode. Michigan in 1892 chose twelve Electors by districts and two by super-districts, one of the two being chosen by the eastern, the other by the western part of the state; this re-establishment of the district system was occasioned by the desire of the Democratic legislature to salvage a few electoral votes from the wreck which it saw to be impending.

These exceptions out of the general rule are worthy of notice since they prove that the faculty of change still exists. The third is of particular interest, for it tends to prove that the faculty of change cannot, under present conditions, be exercised otherwise than abusively. The demonstration of this proposition, however, I reserve to a later chapter.

The disappearance of every mode of appointment but the general ticket weakened the cause of the reformers. Their leading argument was turned against them. "I grant," said Edward Everett of Massachusetts answering McDuffie in the great debate of 1826, "to the gentleman from South Carolina that diversity, in this respect, is an evil. It is an evil that one State should appoint its Electors in one way, and another State in another way. I admit that this is an evil for which a remedy is desirable; though I do not know—if no other remedy could be applied—whether it would be ex-

[43] "The Republican party had secured control of the state government. They intended not to risk this control, but to withdraw from the realm of uncertainty the electoral vote of Florida. Accordingly the legislature enacted a law on August the 6th which left to the joint action of the Senate and House the choice of presidential electors" (William Watson Davis, *The Civil War and Reconstruction in Florida* [New York, 1913], p. 540).

pedient (if it were competent to us) to alter the Constitution for this purpose. But the gentleman himself tells us that there is another remedy. He says that, as the Constitution now is, without any alteration, the States will all be led to adopt the General Ticket system. What more do we want, as far as uniformity goes? If the States will all adopt the General Ticket system, without any amendment to the Constitution, then the only evil which I admit to exist, is remedied." [44]

The debate was forced into another channel. The question, it was said, turned upon the relative advantages of the general ticket and district modes of voting. The district system was the true system, that to which the people were attached because it rendered their elective franchise efficient; but it could be established only by constitutional amendment. In defect of such an amendment the general ticket system, the worst plan, must prevail, from a sort of state necessity, in opposition to the sentiments of the people. There was a great difference between a uniformity imposed by necessity and one adopted by choice. The first uniformity would deliver up the votes of the state to the active managers in the General Assemblies; the second would leave them in the hands of the real sovereigns, the qualified voters of the whole state. [45]

But the people were no longer listening. As the district system went out of use and the general ticket system became familiar it was ominously noticed that the people were beginning to look upon the latter mode of election almost without disapprobation. [46] Presently, they came to regard it as a

---

[44] II *Register of Debates*, 1575.

[45] 41 *Annals*, 1073; II *Register of Debates*, Appendix, p. 127.

[46] Senator Dickerson observed the fact as early as 1818 (31 *Annals*, 186).

natural system, even to venerate it as sanctioned by custom. Today, it is probable that the vast majority of the people suppose the general ticket to be prescribed, not merely permitted, by the Constitution. Thus has it happened that a manner of appointment which owes its establishment to the ferocity of party politics and the demoralizing institutions of faction can nowadays be represented to the people, falsely but without fear of discovery, as the manner sanctified by the approbation of the Founding Fathers.

Part Two

PRESENT VIEW AND PROSPECT

4. The General Ticket Plurality System

The Electoral College is the body which in law chooses the President or, in certain contingencies, nominates to the House of Representatives the candidates from amongst whom the President shall be chosen. At present the whole number of Electors is five hundred and thirty-one. Of these, ninety-six are distributed among the states according to the principle of state equality, each state being entitled to two. The remaining four hundred and thirty-five are distributed according to the principle of population, each state being entitled to as many Electors as it has Representatives in Congress. Congress can, if it will, vary the relative weight of the states in the Electoral College by increasing or diminishing the whole number of Representatives; the smaller the House, the smaller the proportion of Electors chosen by the numerical principle; but the census alone governs the apportionment among the states of the major number of Electors. And in the census everyone is counted: men, women, and children; black men, white men, brown men, yellow men, and red men; citizens and aliens; Catholics, Protestants, Jews, Buddhists, and atheists; Democrats, Republicans, Socialists, and Communists; gypsies and stay-at-homes; rebels and patriots; criminals and law-abiding persons; idiots, lunatics, and sane men. In particular, no discrimination is made between voters and non-voters. The right of representation is not based on, and has no relation to, the right of suffrage.

Two exceptions must be made to this rule, but neither of them is of the slightest practical importance. First, the Constitution has excluded from the basis of apportionment all "Indians not taxed." These are the Indians resident within the boundaries of a state but not subject to its ordinary jurisdiction. The Director of the Census has declared that no such Indians now exist, and accordingly none are reported. Second, the Fourteenth Amendment, section 2, has provided for a reduction in the representation of any state which discriminates in its suffrage laws against any of its male, adult citizens, with certain exceptions. This part of the amendment, intended to deprive the Southern states of their Negro representation, has never been enforced, and was probably superseded by the Fifteenth Amendment, absolutely forbidding discrimination on account of race, color, or previous condition of servitude. A fee for doing what is permissible is not the same thing as a penalty for doing what is forbidden.

In the organization of the Electoral College no distinction is drawn between the Electors given to the states on the basis of state equality and those given to them on the basis of relative population. The Electors, though meeting in separate places,[1] are not divided, like Congress, into two Houses, each with a reciprocal negative upon the other. They form a single body; each Elector has one vote; the concurrence of a majority of the whole number of Electors appointed is requisite

[1] "The Electors shall meet in their respective States" (*U.S. Constitution*, Art. II, sec. 1).

to a definitive choice; a full appointment being assumed, any two hundred sixty-six Electors can make a President; if some state should neglect to appoint Electors—as did New York in 1789—a smaller number would suffice. If no candidate for President receives the requisite majority of electoral votes, the election is completed by the House of Representatives, that body being confined in its choice to the persons having the three highest numbers on the list of those voted for by the Electors.

Each state is authorized by the Constitution to appoint the Electors allocated to it "in such manner as the legislature thereof may direct." No mode or range of modes is prescribed by the Constitution; none is forbidden. But, as we have seen, every state, for many years past, has appointed its Electors by the general ticket plurality system. The general ticket plurality system is a device for concentrating the electoral suffrages of a state upon a single person, regardless of the sentiments of divisions. Under it every voter in a state is invited to vote for every Elector to which the state is entitled; since a plurality is sufficient to elect, and since an individual voter has no real choice but to vote for a list of Electors previously manufactured by a political party,[2] it follows almost automatically that the political party with the greatest number of popular votes in the state at large secures the appointment of its entire slate of Electors, and consequently secures the whole number of the state's electoral votes for its presidential candidate.

Almost automatically, but not quite. In states which require or permit the voters to cast a distinct vote for each individual Elector, it may happen that, in a close contest, some Electors may be chosen from one ticket and some from an-

[2] See page 59.

other. In 1796, for example, in Pennsylvania, the highest Republican candidate for Elector and the highest Federalist candidate were separated by only 89 votes; the two general tickets overlapped, and the Federalists secured the appointment of two of the state's fifteen Electors.[3] In 1892 the leading Cleveland Elector in Ohio received more votes than the leading Harrison Elector, and was appointed; but the other twenty-two Cleveland Electors were defeated. In the same year, in North Dakota, one Elector was appointed from the Harrison ticket and two from the Cleveland-Weaver fusion ticket. In 1904 and again in 1908 Maryland divided its vote; in 1904 it chose one Roosevelt and seven Parker Electors; in 1908, two Taft and six Bryan Electors. In 1916 West Virginia appointed one Elector from the Wilson ticket and seven from the Hughes ticket. Upon three separate occasions the California voters split their electoral tickets with similar results. In 1880 they gave one Elector to Hancock and the others to Garfield; in 1892, one to Harrison and the others to Cleveland; in 1912, two to Wilson and the others to Roosevelt.

Such results are the consequence of various causes. Personal feeling plays its part. An unusually popular candidate may run ahead of his ticket; an obnoxious one behind it.[4] Why a voter should allow himself to be cheated of his purpose to vote for the presidential candidate of his choice merely because he has a dislike for an Elector who has merely a perfunctory duty to perform in the machinery of election, may be, as the editors of the *Century Magazine* once declared

[3] One of these two (Samuel Miles) later voted against his party.

[4] "In New York State, in 1892, Richard Croker, the boss of Tammany Hall, received a smaller number of votes as elector than any other man on the Cleveland electoral ticket. This was obviously due to dislike of Tammany Hall, without regard to the merits of presidential candidates." (45 *Century Magazine*, 794.)

it to be, a mystery; yet history proves that wherever split-ticket voting is permitted, the names of Electors on every ticket are scratched by hundreds and sometimes thousands of voters.[5] Voter-fatigue is another factor. It has long been noticed that the candidates whose names appear at the bottom of a party's list of Electors receive fewer votes than those whose names appear at the top. The Pennsylvania division of 1796 and the California division of 1912 ought probably to be attributed to this cause. So, too, should the California division of 1892; in that year the defeated Cleveland Elector, a man by the name of Thompson, stood last on the Democratic list; the successful Harrison Elector stood first on the Republican list; Thompson, with much reason, pointed to the alphabet as the cause of his defeat.[6] Voter-confusion must also be taken into account. In the Ohio division of 1892 and the Maryland division of 1904 a change in the method of marking ballots had left many voters under the impression that a mark against the first name, or indeed any name on an electoral list, would be counted as a vote for every name; it is very probable that without this misunderstanding the entire Cleveland ticket in Ohio and the entire Roosevelt ticket in Maryland would have been in. Finally, there is the case of error. The North Dakota division of 1892 is said to have been due to a mistake in the final count that was not rectified until after the result had been officially proclaimed by the Governor and could not be altered.[7]

Not only may the largest party in a state lose some of its Electors under the general ticket system; it may, in exceptional circumstances, lose all of them. In 1824 the voters of North Carolina were asked to choose between three presi-

[5] *Ibid.*
[6] 46 *Century Magazine*, 157-158.
[7] 45 *Century Magazine*, 794.

dential candidates—Crawford, Jackson, and Adams—but they were presented with only two electoral tickets, one pledged to Crawford, the other (in effect) pledged against him. The supporters of Jackson and Adams, by the manufacture of a coalition ticket, produced a factitious but absolute majority in the state which defeated the real but relative majority that, presumably, favored Crawford. In 1892 and 1896 similar combinations were made in many states against the party presumed to be the strongest. Sometimes the Democrats and Populists combined with intent to defeat the Republicans; sometimes the Republicans and Populists combined with intent to defeat the Democrats.

It is even conceivable that under the present system a presidential candidate favored by an absolute majority of the people of a state may receive none of that state's electoral votes. If one candidate is supported by two or more parties with distinct slates of Electors, only the votes cast for the largest of these parties can be of avail to him. The contest, it must always be borne in mind, is not between presidential candidates but between slates of Electors pledged to presidential candidates. Factional tickets, tickets favoring the same man but with different Electors, can serve only to defeat the popular will. No instance can be cited in which a candidate has lost the electoral votes of a whole state because of the division of his popular vote between two or more electoral slates, but an incident taken from the history of Maryland, much noticed at the time of its occurrence, will serve to illustrate the point. At the election of 1824 the people of Maryland, voting by districts, appointed the Electors. In one district there were two candidates for Elector in favor of Adams and one in favor of Jackson. A majority of the people in the district favored Adams, but their votes were so distracted between his two Electors that the Jackson Elector received a plurality and was appointed. What can happen in a single district can happen in the state at large. Cases in which distinct general tickets have been pledged to the same presidential candidate are rare, but not unknown. At the election of 1812 two separate tickets were introduced in Ohio, both purporting to be for Madison; one was spurious and had the effect of diverting from Madison a part, though only a small part, of his support.[8] At the election of 1892 Harrison was favored by two separate tickets in Alabama and by two in Texas. At the election of 1896 there were two distinct McKinley tickets in Louisiana, Mississippi, and South Carolina; and in several states there were two or more distinct Bryan tickets.

These variations, deviations, aberrations, from the ordinary course of action contemplated by the general ticket plurality system ought probably to be considered as defects of that system. An individual voter can only weaken the effectiveness of his vote by splitting or "scratching" his electoral ticket. A group of voters favorable to a single candidate do him no favor by distracting his strength between two or more slates of Electors. A combination of political groups favorable to different candidates but primarily opposed to one may be justifiable when that one is truly obnoxious to the community as a whole, but when the combination is no more than a political juggle designed to strip the plurality candidate of his prize, not much can be said for it.

All these difficulties could, of course, be avoided without disturbing the general ticket plurality system. The simplest remedy, and one that has often been proposed, would be to abolish the intermediate Electors, to authorize the qualified

---

[8] 26 *Annals*, 833; 3 *Niles' Register*, 208. The regular Madison (Anti-Tammany) ticket received 7,420 votes; the spurious ticket about 1,000.

voters in each state to vote directly for the President, and to provide that the person receiving the greatest number of votes for President in each state should be credited with the whole number of electoral votes to which that state is entitled. But such a remedy could be ordained only by an amendment to the Constitution. It is useless to discuss it, for there is an antecedent question to be considered: Is the general ticket system itself a proper mode of electing the President? If our answer to this question is in the negative, as it must be, then the idea of smoothing the anomalies of the general ticket system by constitutional amendment becomes improper. Let us do what we can by state laws, but let us leave the Constitution alone. The amending process is a necessary and valuable institution, but it ought to be used to remove evil, not to confirm and normalize it.

Many strong arguments have been brought to bear against the general ticket system during the hundred and sixty-odd years that it has been under attack. Before examining them, it may be well to remind the reader once again of the inherent instability of that system. The faculty of change is reserved by the Constitution to the state legislatures respectively. It is entirely conceivable that a majority in a state legislature, anticipating an unfavorable outcome to the next election, might attempt to fortify itself against the event by changing the mode of appointing Electors; what Michigan did in 1892 some other state might do in 1960 or in 1980. Nor can we expect such an abuse of power always to be reprobated by the constituents of the state legislators. Much will depend on the manner in which the state senatorial and assembly districts are drawn; an arrangement which permits the minority party in a state to elect a majority in the legislature will also permit that majority to defy the general will with a certain impunity. Much also will depend on the relationships of the various classes of society admitted to exercise the right of suffrage; circumstances can be imagined, especially in the Southern states, where a change from the general ticket system to, let us say, the legislative choice or the gerrymandering system might even be applauded by the dominant majority.

That instability is an evil, is a proposition that few will deny. But it is an evil to be charged to the faculty of change rather than to the general ticket system. To say that the election of the President ought not to be regulated by the diversified and clashing expedients of forty-eight states, mutually independent, is to say only that the mode of choosing that officer should be given the fixedness and permanence of a constitutional rule. What that rule should be is a distinct question.

It has been justly said that the plan of voting by a general ticket is not consistent with the true theory of a popular representation.[9] The President is the man of the people—a phrase that must be read, as the men of 1787 read it, without Napoleonic overtones. The Electoral College was designed by the Founding Fathers as a representation of the people. By basing its numbers on the principle of population rather than on that of state sovereignty, by giving to each Elector a separate vote, instead of to each state a consolidated vote composed of all its electoral suffrages, they clearly intended to give to each mass of persons entitled to one Elector the right of giving one vote for President according to its own sense of its own interests.[10] In a small state it is very probable that the interests of every man may coincide, but in a large state it is even more probable that they will diverge. Some sections will be agricultural, some manufacturing, and some

[9] Report of the McDuffie Committee, House of Representatives, December, 1823 (41 *Annals*, 855).

[10] 41 *Annals*, 169 (Senator Benton of Missouri).

commercial; some Republican, some Democratic, some perhaps of a third or fourth party. All these interests and opinions were meant to be represented in the Electoral College: None was to be disenfranchised nor deprived of its voice in the election of a President.

Even the two extra Electors allotted to each state without regard to population can hardly be said to have been given on the federative principle; they are to be explained as a corrective to the anticipated influence of state favoritism, an influence which it was feared would give the separate masses in the large states an advantage over those in small ones. The federative principle would have required these extra Electors to be organized, like the Senate, as a separate house with a veto on the popular representation.

Nor can we say that time has brought about a change in the intention of the Constitution. The comparisons that are made every four years between the distribution of the popular vote and that of the electoral vote; the fear universally expressed that the man who stands first in the popular count may stand second in the electoral count; the necessity that impels the defenders of the general ticket system to explain away the results of the Hayes-Tilden and Harrison-Cleveland elections, and the advocates of reform to pretend that their own systems would absolutely prevent anyone but the man favored by the greatest number of popular votes from obtaining a majority of the electoral votes—all these things go to prove that the Constitution means now what it meant in the beginning: that the election of the President is not a state but a national question; that, in determining it, all the people of the Union are to stand upon the same footing; that the interests of every equal mass of persons entitled to one Elector, regardless of its location in one state or another, are to have a full and efficient voice.

And how is the theory of the Constitution to be reconciled with the practice of the general ticket system? That system is based on the federative and not the popular principle. Unequal masses of persons are given unequal numbers of electoral votes to be cast in blocks. The representation of each state in the Electoral College is not even intended to be a local representation of the sentiments of its people; for it is always unanimous. New York is a great state, very evenly divided in its political opinions; it is entitled to forty-three Representatives in Congress and to forty-five Electors. Let it be assumed that in a presidential year it sends twenty-one Democrats and twenty-two Republicans to Congress; in the same year it will send, as accident may determine, forty-five Democrats or forty-five Republicans to the Electoral College. The general ticket system, in short, makes the President the man of the states and not the man of the people.

Judged by the popular principle, the general ticket system can only be pronounced unfair. It commits the choice of the President, not to the people of the Union as a whole, but to the people of the large states, as such. The point can be made clear by an example. New York has 45 electoral votes and Pennsylvania 32; let it be supposed that the sense of the people of New York is divided between the Republican and the Democratic candidates in the proportion of 23 to 22, while the sense of Pennsylvania is unanimous for the Republican. In this state of things, what is the voice of the people in those states? And what would be the estimated vote by the general ticket system? The candidate who was fairly entitled to count 54 electoral votes would actually receive only 32, while his opponent, entitled to 23, would receive 45. The case put is an extreme one, but that fact does not weaken its force as an illustration of the point we are making. If the result of an election depended on the action of New York and Pennsylvania alone, it is plain that nothing would matter but the distribution of popular votes in New York; for all the practical effect they could have on the election, the Pennsylvania voters might just as well stay home. At the present time the dominant pluralities in the eleven largest states control 264 electoral votes; if, with one other state, they should give their votes to a single candidate, he would be elected regardless of the strength of his opposition in those states and the rest of the Union together. But it needs no elaborate calculation to show that the candidate of the majority of the people of the Union is far from certain to prevail in an Electoral College where the representation of each state is not that of its people but of its dominant plurality.

The inequity of the general ticket system can be demonstrated in a number of other ways. The whole of the New England states make a district less populous and better integrated than the state of New York. Would the people of any of these states—say Maine or Vermont—consent to be placed in a single New England district with a general ticket? If they would not—and everyone knows they would not— is it just to hold New York in her present situation, a situation that in practice compels the annihilation of the up-state voters by the down-state voters or vice versa?

Annihilation, indeed, is too weak a word. "To lose their votes," said Benton of Missouri, "is the fate of all minorities, and it is their duty to submit; but this is not a case of votes lost, but of votes taken away, added to those of the majority, and given to a person to whom the minority is opposed." [11] In New York the quantum of population entitled to one Elector may be put at 350,000 persons. New York appoints forty-five electors; twenty-three is a majority, and the candidate

[11] 41 *Annals*, 170 (1824).

receiving this majority is fairly entitled to count 23 electoral votes; but he counts in reality 45, because the minority of 22 is added to the majority. These 22 votes belong to twenty-two masses of people, of 350,000 souls each, in all 7,700,000 people, whose votes are seized upon, taken away, and presented to whom the majority pleases. As McDuffie of South Carolina remarked, the general ticket system gives the votes of these millions of people to the candidate *against* whom they actually voted: "The very votes which the *People* intended to defeat his election, are, by the *State*, wrested from their legitimate aim, and made subservient to the advancement of a man, who may, perhaps, be an object of abhorrence to the very People who are thus compelled into his service." [12]

This line of attack on the general ticket system has never been answered; it is indeed unanswerable. Attempts have sometimes been made to liken each of the state segments of a presidential election to the whole of a gubernatorial election; in the latter the votes of the entire state minority are of course lost, and the winner takes the whole prize. But McDuffie's reply is conclusive: "We are led into error, on this subject of minorities, by not distinguishing between things that are essentially different. Wherever the action of a State is final and conclusive upon a subject, as in the election of her own Governor, the minority must of course submit; but, where the action of all the States of the Union is directed to one common result, the election of a President, the respective State minorities should be brought into the calculation, that we may really ascertain who has the genuine majority of the whole.[13] Besides, there is no analogy between the ordinary mode of electing a Governor and the present mode of electing a President. When a Governor is elected by the people, a candidate does not count

[12] II *Register of Debates*, 1370 (1826).
[13] *Ibid.*

the unanimous vote of every county where he may happen to obtain a plurality; on the contrary, the respective pluralities of the several candidates are added to their respective minorities and the aggregates thus produced are taken as the true expression of the popular will.[14] The popular principle rules the election of a Governor; it cannot be pointed to as a justification for using the federative principle in the election of a President.

That the general ticket system is grounded on a wrong idea, violates the rights of minorities, and makes the President the representative of the states and not of the people, are the great objections that have always been urged against its preservation. But habit takes the edge off principle. Familiarity with the system together with the correspondence that in recent elections, most of which have been national landslides, has undoubtedly subsisted between the will of the states and the will of the people has reduced the force of these objections but has not affected their validity. All we can say is that the statesmen who lived when the general ticket system was being established had a truer and a clearer view of its real meaning than the statesmen who now gain or suffer from its operation. Chief Justice John Marshall stated in 1828 that "he had not voted since the establishment of the general ticket system and had believed that he would not vote during its continuance" [15]—a pretty clear indication of his opinion of its equity. Marshall was a Virginia Federalist. Madison, on the other hand, was a Republican. In 1800 he worked to bring about the adoption by Virginia of the gen-

---

[14] A House Committee made this point in 1823 (41 *Annals*, 860); as did James K. Polk in 1826 (II *Register of Debates*, 1649).

[15] Albert J. Beveridge, *Life of John Marshall* (Boston, 1919), IV, 263-264. Marshall thought that he would probably depart from his resolution in 1828, in order to vote against General Jackson.

eral ticket system, but on the question of equity his views were the same as Marshall's. He sustained a system that he knew to be unfair, on the single basis of retributive justice, but throughout his life he never ceased to denounce its absolute error and to recommend its replacement by a national, uniform district system. Marshall and Madison may fairly be taken as reflecting, respectively, the opinions, not of the Federalists and Republicans, but of the minorities and majorities, whatever their political complexion, in the several states. Both sides agreed that the general ticket system was improper, but the dominant party excused its establishment "as the only expedient for baffling the policy of the particular States which had set the example." [16]

Besides its inequity, the general ticket system has other evils. It puts a premium on fraud. The presidency is a great prize; the anticipated patronage of the Executive is an inducement to designing men to offer corrupt influence; the strength of this inducement is proportional to the number of electoral votes that can be affected by such influence. In the large doubtful states, particularly, politicians play for high stakes. Let it be supposed that in New York the gaining of a single influential individual will turn the scale; the swing in the Electoral College will be 90 votes, enough to decide many an election; anyone can see that, in such a balance of parties, the temptations to intrigue are enormous and that the general ticket system is admirably calculated to promote the schemes of ambition. Senator Dickerson of New Jersey put the point very well nearly one hundred and forty years ago, when he advocated the replacement of the general ticket by the district system: "In proportion as we diminish the circle upon which intrigue is to act, in the same proportion do we add to the

[16] Madison to George Hay, August 23, 1823 (Madison, *Writings*, IX, 151-152).

force and energy of that intrigue. . . . The force of intrigue, which would produce no sensible effect upon two hundred and twenty-one districts, would be irresistible when applied to a single point." [17]

It will scarcely be thought necessary to give examples of corruption. The reader, however, may recall that in 1868, when the sense of the nation was preponderantly in favor of Grant, New York gave her 33 votes to Seymour. That state was controlled by the Tweed Ring, a group of active political managers not conspicuous for their virtue; the difference in the popular vote for the two candidates was exactly 10,000 (out of an aggregate of nearly 850,000); and it was generally understood that this result had been brought about by fraud.[18] In this instance the alleged fraud had no effect upon the national election. But in 1876 the case was different; the Republican returning boards in Louisiana, South Carolina, and Florida played their parts in the election of Hayes over Tilden.

It has been said in answer to this argument that the effects of fraud are immaterial to the welfare of the country: Where two candidates contend for the presidency, each possessing the qualifications necessary for the high station, it can make no serious difference to the Union which of the two should succeed. But this answer misses the point. The danger is not that the affairs of our government will be administered by the second, instead of the first, man in the Union, between whom there may be no great difference in point of honor, integrity, talent, or information, but that the people may

[17] 33 *Annals,* 144 (1819).

[18] "This result, it was believed by many persons, was brought about intentionally, with a view to saving certain large wagers upon the Democratic majority in New York" (Edward Stanwood, *A History of the Presidency* [New York, 1912], p. 329).

reject the authority of a president who owes his office principally to intrigue, cabal, and management. Doubtless no system of election could wholly exclude intrigue or place the choice of the President upon the footing of a completely free and unbiased expression of the public will; but the general ticket system is among the worst that could be devised. Its tendency is to render the presidential election less rather than more free and independent; to deliver it into, rather than remove it from, the grasp of party arrangements; to promote rather than prevent bargains between profligate agents and the selling of the nation for offices to the highest bidder.

Apart from fraud, the general ticket system puts a premium on accident. In a state where the division of parties is approximately equal, great effects will result from small causes. Stormy weather may keep rural voters from the polls; local issues may bring out voters in some particular districts in unusual numbers; any of the thousand casualties of political fortune may determine the column in which a state's electoral vote will be found. In 1844 Silas Wright was persuaded to run for Governor of New York; the gubernatorial and presidential campaigns were conducted as one; Wright brought to Polk more than the 5,000 votes by which he carried the state; New York's 36 electoral votes determined the election. But for the intervention of Wright, Clay would have been President. In 1848 the electoral votes of New York were again decisive; but they were given to Taylor rather than Cass, only because Van Buren, running for President on the Free Soil ticket, had split the Democratic party. It is to the hazards of political arithmetic that we must attribute the election of Harrison in 1888; in carrying the large states by small pluralities and losing the small states by large pluralities, he turned a deficit of 96,000 popular votes into a surplus of 65 electoral votes. In 1916 a political mistake in California by Hughes gave the electoral votes of that state, and with them the presidency, to Wilson. In 1948 the supporters of Henry Wallace split the Democratic party in New York and threw that state with its 47 electoral votes from Truman to Dewey, but without effect on the national outcome. As a Southern statesman once remarked: "These sudden and sweeping vibrations, depending upon such small and inadequate causes, are alone sufficient to demonstrate the defectiveness of the system that gives rise to them." [19]

The general ticket system may also be criticized on the ground that it blows up the bargaining power of splinter parties and pressure groups in the large doubtful states beyond all reason. Let it be supposed that, at a given election, the sentiments of the people of New York are divided in such a way that, by the principle of numbers, the Democrats would be entitled to 22 electoral votes, the Republicans to 22, and the American Labor party to 1. Let it further be supposed that the American Labor party, knowing that it cannot elect a President of its own, decides to support the nominee of one of the great parties. Very naturally, and indeed properly, it will hawk its strength at market, promising its popular votes to the party which will give it the greatest assurances that its grievances will be removed or its interests advanced. No mode of election can prevent such bargaining. But, under the general ticket mode, what has the American Labor party to offer? In the case supposed, not merely the single electoral vote to which it is justly entitled, but the 22 Democratic or Republican votes, as the case may be, which it will take away from the person for whom they were intended, and present to the person for whom they were not intended. What any minor political party can do can also be done, though with greater difficulty, by any well-organized ethnic,

[19] II *Register of Debates*, 1373 (McDuffie).

religious, social, or economic group. The advantage of the former lies solely in the fact that it can direct the votes of its constituents into the desired channel by presenting them with an electoral ticket made up of the same persons that compose the ticket of the major party to be aided; non-political groups must rely on influence alone.

The real gravamen of this charge against the general ticket system has been much obscured in debate, both by the advocates and by the opponents of reform. The merits of the Negro question, the Zionist question, the Catholic question, the labor-management question, the Communist question, have been dragged into the controversy. We are told that the disproportionate power wielded in the large doubtful states by small masses of persons is a valuable instrument of reform or a dangerous instrument of oppression; that the bargains struck are good or bad. But the point is irrelevant. If the President is to be the man of the people, if all the people are to stand on the same footing, equal masses of people must be given equal votes, equal bargaining power. Their weight in the electoral count must be proportional to their numbers and not to the rightness or wrongness of their causes. The idea of distinguishing good groups from bad groups and assigning a greater electoral weight to the former than the latter is without merit; nor can it be reduced to practice.

Let us turn to an objection of another type. It was noticed at an early date that the tendency of the general ticket system is to promote and strengthen sectionalism in our party arrangements. Let the mode of voting be such as to make the election of the President spring from the cooperation of individuals for a common purpose in different parts of the Union, and a connection will be created between the general government and themselves that will weaken the violence of local feelings and local prejudices. The citizens of one extreme uniting with the citizens of another extreme of the Union, to promote the election of the same individual as the President of their country, will be drawn to each other as members of the same political family. They will feel the sentiment of a common country. Their joint exertions, in their individual capacities, must create one of the strongest bonds of union. But let the mode of voting be such as to throw the entire vote of each state into the scale of its favorite candidate, and though a cooperation will be brought about between state and state, or in other words, a cooperation between the leaders of one state and those of another, the people of the nation will be disunited and broken into distinct masses. "Such a cooperation of State with State," said a Southern Congressman with singular prescience in 1814, "far from being productive of benefit to the nation, is scarcely less to be dreaded than the array of State against State. Both the one and the other are full of danger—while the opposition of individuals is harmless, and their union most salutary." [20]

Comparing the general ticket system with the district system in 1823, Madison had this to say: "The States, when voting for President by general tickets or by their Legislatures, are a string of beads; when they make their elections by districts, some of these differing in sentiment from others, and sympathizing with that of districts in other States, they are so knit together as to break the force of those geographical and other noxious parties which might render the repulsive too strong for the cohesive tendencies within the political system." [21] Madison was both echoing and anticipating the opinions of other statesmen. The suppression of minorities, Senator Dickerson of New Jersey had said in 1818 and again

[20] 26 *Annals*, 841 (Israel Pickens of North Carolina).
[21] Madison to George Hay, August 23, 1823 (Madison, *Writings*, IX, 152).

in 1819, must increase the rancor and bitterness of party, exhibit the states in a sort of hostile array against each other, and cherish the uncharitable, social, and clannish disposition to which must be ascribed no small share of the embarrassments and calamities which our government had theretofore experienced.[22] "A further mischief of the general ticket system," another Senator was to say in 1824, "is, in segregating the States, drawing them up against one another, like hostile ships in battle. Out of this system has sprung the anti-social words of modern invention—'effective votes,' 'operative votes'—as if the States were contending with Turks or Russians. This alienates the States from each other, and fills them with hostile feelings, and the President elected must become the President of the States which choose him, and look with coldness and resentment upon those which opposed him." [23]

It was further perceived that the combinations of states facing each other at each election were not random but geographical. The distribution of electoral votes in 1812 was deeply disturbing to all the friends of union, to all those who thought that the citizens of the Republic, though divided into states for certain essential purposes, were one people in all that related to the general government. In that year the states north and east of Pennsylvania and Maryland, with the exception of one small state, were, by the manner of voting, unanimously opposed to the election of the candidate who succeeded; while the states south and west were unanimously in his favor. Two years later Representative Pickens of North Carolina sounded a warning: "When the States give an entire vote it may frequently happen that each end of the Union will give a united vote in opposition to the other, as was nearly the case at the last Presidential elec-

---

[22] 31 *Annals*, 187; 33 *Annals*, 143.
[23] 41 *Annals*, 170 (Benton).

tion. This happening to be the case habitually for a few periods, the political parties will gradually assume a geographical character. A man elected by the entire votes of one end of the Union will be looked at by the other end not as the representative of the nation, but rather as the head of the party, and that party a local sectional one." [24]

Representative McDuffie of South Carolina elaborated this argument in 1826 in a speech recommending the restoration of the district system by constitutional amendment: "Every friend of the Union cannot but perceive a strong objection to the general ticket system, in its tendency to form political parties upon the basis of geographical arrangement. By bringing large political masses into the Presidential contest, by arraying State against State in the consolidated energy of their power, feelings and passions unfriendly to the harmony of the Union will be unavoidably generated. It is a fact known to us all, that, in almost every portion of the Union, there is a local feeling, which is but too apt to enter into all political questions affecting the general interests of the Republic. Into no question is this feeling more likely to infuse itself than that of the election of the Chief Magistrate. From this influence it will generally be found that the majority of the People in every State will give their support to the candidate residing in their own particular section of the Union. But there will generally be a minority, respectable in point of numbers, and still more so in point of wisdom and virtue, that will rise superior to local predilections, and look exclusively to the promotion of the national welfare. The unavoidable effect of the general ticket system is to render the sectional feeling, to which I have alluded, omnipotent, by entirely excluding the vote of the high-minded minority that

[24] 26 *Annals*, 832.

would be disposed to resist it. The district system, by giving to this minority its legitimate weight in the election, would tend to put down the pretensions of those political aspirants who could only hope for success by enlisting local prejudices in their favor." [25]

These were not simply the views of isolated statesmen. In 1823 a committee of the House of Representatives, after noting that the inevitable tendency of the general ticket system was to produce a geographical formation of parties, declared that if the system were continued, "we need not the prophetic spirit of Washington to warn us that the harmony of the Union would be destroyed, and perhaps its existence endangered." [26]

It is doubtless true that, nowadays, the force of these arguments is much diminished. The great social question which divided the nation before the Civil War has been decided; the cohesive tendencies of our political system have proved stronger than the repulsive; the sentiments of loyalty and affection that bind the citizens to the general government are perhaps now stronger than those that bind them to their common state. Nevertheless, sectionalism persists. There are, in truth, no great national parties, only sectional alliances of state parties. Statesmen would do well to ask themselves, thinking particularly of the people in the Solid South, whether the abolition of the general ticket system might not help to diminish the implacability and acrimony of sectional feeling.

Another objection to the general ticket system is that it produces a kind of political apathy in the so-called safe states. If opposition is necessary in a free country, opposition should be kept alive. But in a state that is preponderantly Republican or preponderantly Democratic, opposition is stifled. The

[25] II *Register of Debates*, 1370-1371.
[26] 41 *Annals*, 855.

minority voters do not bother to go to the polls because they know that their votes cannot be effective. Their indifference is shared by the majority voters; these stay home because they know that their votes are not needed.

Finally, it can be argued that the general ticket system has an adverse effect on the choice of candidates by the great political parties. In a political convention the inquiry is never who could carry the country as a whole but who could carry New York, Pennsylvania, California, and the other large doubtful states. No doubt it often happens that the sense of the people in the large doubtful states corresponds with the sense of the people in the nation at large. But the correspondence is uncertain. And it is contrary to the spirit of our institutions that the sense of a minority should prevail over that of the majority.

All these objections, taken together, prove, I submit, that the course of things under the present mode of choosing a President is in its nature pernicious and tends to prevent the object, intended by the Constitution, of a pure elective magistracy. Rufus King, a member of the Federal Convention, so pronounced it in 1816; [27] his words are equally true today.

[27] 29 *Annals*, 223.

5. The National Plebiscite System

The simplest remedy for the manifest evils of the general ticket system, the easiest to understand, and, at first blush, the fairest-seeming is undoubtedly that which is currently being advocated by Senator William Langer of North Dakota, former Senator Herbert H. Lehman of New York, and a number of other statesmen. Let the whole machinery of electoral voting be struck from the Constitution—the electoral votes as well as the intermediate Electors who cast them—and let the choice of the President be made to depend on the direct votes of the people in the nation at large. Let each individual voter name the person whom he wishes to be President; let all the votes of all the voters be collected in one general return; and let the election be decreed to him who has a majority of the whole.[1]

[1] There is a division of opinion as to what should be done if no candidate has a majority. Some would permit a plurality to elect; others would require a run-off election in certain contingencies; but all would agree that in any run-off election the choice should be confined to the two or three persons standing highest in the popular vote. The national plebiscite system, in short, contemplates that the

The merits of this scheme may seem almost immediately obvious. If the President is to be the man of the people, why should he not be elected immediately by the people? And if he is to be elected immediately by the people, why should not every individual voter stand upon the same footing? "The plain and obvious principle of representation," said Senator John Sherman of Ohio in 1866, "is that every voter should vote for himself and for no one else." [2] One voter, one vote: That is the underlying, apparently unchallengeable idea of the national plebiscite system.

That system would sweep away at once all the difficulties and evils that have been alleged against the present method. It would fix the election of the President on a uniform principle, not susceptible of alteration by the several state legislatures. It would make that principle national rather than federative. It would prevent the large states from consolidating their votes to the disadvantage and oppression of the small ones. It would protect the rights of minorities in every state. It would reduce the premium on fraud and accident. It would make the electoral power of splinter parties and pressure groups more nearly proportional to their numbers. It would prevent slight changes in the political sentiments of a state from producing sudden and entire revolutions in its political character. It would promote political activity in the so-called safe states— the states of homogeneous sentiment. It would affect the choice of candidates by the national conventions of the major parties, causing them to seek out the man of the nation rather than the man of the great doubtful states. It would inspire sentiments of nationality among the whole body of the people: "What," asked one of the earliest advocates of the

people at large will either make the President immediately or name the candidates from whom the President shall be made.

[2] *Congressional Globe*, 39th Cong., 1st sess., p. 2986.

national plebiscite system, "could make us so much one people, as to give all the people this general equal privilege? It will produce in the national habits, manners, and love of country, more harmony than any other political measure which could be possibly adopted." [3]

This list of merits is impressive and could be extended. But it is useless to go on. The national plebiscite system has one great handicap that cannot be overcome. It could be established only by constitutional amendment, and no amendment establishing it stands any chance whatever of passing the Senate or being adopted by the states. The difficulty can be briefly stated. The national plebiscite system would completely alter the relative weights of the several states in the election of the President. These are now determined by the Constitution according to a formula in which the only variable is population—total population, comprising voters and non-voters alike. The national plebiscite system, in any given election, would make those weights depend solely on the number of votes cast and counted.

Anyone who will trouble himself to make up a table comparing the relative weights of the states under the two systems will immediately perceive the difficulty. Let him in one column arrange the states in order of population, according to the census of 1950, and calculate their present weight in the Electoral College as percentages of the whole; let him in another column arrange them in order of number of votes cast at the election of 1952 and calculate their presumptive weights under the national plebiscite system. The comparison will be instructive. It will be seen that of the twenty-four smaller states only two, Oklahoma and Connecticut, would gain by a change from the electoral voting to the

[3] 29 *Annals*, 225 (Senator Abner Lacock in 1816).

popular voting system. Oregon would maintain its weight. All
the rest would lose. In the case of the twenty-four larger
states, fourteen would become heavier and ten lighter; all of
these ten lie in the South.

A complete comparison will reveal three important points.
The change of system would result in a shift of weight from
the smaller to the larger states; from the southern section of
the country to the north, east, and west; from states which
are politically passive to those which are politically active.
In 1952, for example, the four largest states cast 136 votes in
the Electoral College; so did the twenty-five smallest states;
but if the basis of representation had been popular votes, the
former would have outweighed the latter by nearly 2 to 1.
In the same year the seven coastal states from Mississippi to
Virginia, inclusive, outweighed the six New England states
in the Electoral College in the ratio of 15 to 8; under the national plebiscite system the weights of the two groups would
have been approximately equal. Again in the same year, Maine
and Vermont cast 8 votes in the Electoral College; Rhode
Island and Delaware cast 7; under the national plebiscite system the relative weights of these two groups, the one more
active than the other, would have been reversed.

These differences are the resultant of several causes, which
may be briefly distinguished. Under the electoral voting system the smallest states (Nevada, Wyoming, Vermont, and
Delaware) acquire two thirds of their weight in the Electoral
College by the two Electors who represent, in that body,
their two Senators. A hundred thousand persons, more or less,
in those states have as much political influence in the election
of the President as 330,000 in New York, which acquires but
two forty-fifths of its weight from this source. Other things
being equal, the national plebiscite system would make the
relative weights of the states in the election of the President

depend solely on their populations. New York with ninety times the numbers of Nevada would have ninety times its weight—instead of fifteen as at present.

But other things are not equal. Different states have different suffrage laws. It has always been noticed that the national plebiscite system would work an injury to the states with the highest requisites for voting. Senator Jeremiah Mason of New Hampshire, for example, in 1816 objected to that system on the ground that the qualifications of voters in the different states were so entirely different that the whole election would be unequal in its bearing on the different states.[4] The Benton Committee in 1826 was careful to point out that its plan of district voting without intermediate Electors was not a plan of consolidation. "Such a plan," it maintained, "would work an injury, not only to the slave-holding States, but in a greater or less degree to almost every State in the Union; for the qualifications of the voters differing in each, some prescribing a freehold possession, some the payment of a tax, some a residence of a few months, others of a year, and others again the privilege of universal suffrage, it would thence result that the same mass of population would yield, in different States, a very unequal number of votes."[5] Nowadays the suffrage laws in the several states are more nearly uniform than they once were, but they are not identical. In most states the franchise is restricted to persons over twenty-one years of age; but in Georgia the voting age is eighteen. In seven states the payment of a poll tax is a prerequisite to voting; in forty-one states it is not. In thirty states illiterates are allowed to vote; in eighteen they are not. Moreover, the literacy test is not the same in all of the states requiring it, and in some, exemptions are granted to persons who own a certain

[4] 29 *Annals*, 223.
[5] II *Register of Debates*, Appendix, p. 125.

quantum of property and have paid a tax on it. A recent writer says very truly that "our medley of voting qualifications operates to curtail the number of voters much more in some states than in others." [6]

But even if the requisites to the right of suffrage were the same in every state, equal masses of population would not produce equal numbers of qualified voters. Everything would depend on the correspondent ratios within each mass of the classes admitted to and the classes excluded from the franchise. In the days of slavery this fact was obvious. "It had pleased God," said a Southern Senator, "to give the Southern country a population anomalous, having the double character of persons and property; other States had none such." [7] Slaves could not vote, but in the basis of representation five slaves counted for three freemen. Had the national plebiscite system prevailed in the election of the President, the Southern states would have lost the privilege allowed them by the Constitution of votes upon three fifths of their population other than freemen. Later on, the difficulty became, if anything, even more obvious. The Thirteenth Amendment abolished slavery. In so doing, it added to the Southern basis of representation two fifths of the former slaves. But it made no change in the suffrage laws. Color was a bar to voting in almost all the states; in the South, in Pennsylvania, and generally in the Western states, it operated as a general exclusion; elsewhere it imposed certain disabilities. But the ratio of Negroes to whites was very different in different sections of the country. In New England the Negro population was so small that its total exclusion from the franchise could make no perceptible difference in its ratio of qualified voters to total population.

[6] Dudley O. McGovney, *The American Suffrage Medley* (Chicago, 1949), p. 9.
[7] 29 *Annals*, 226 (James Barbour of Virginia).

But in the South and West, where Negroes were numbered "by thousands and millions," [8] the case was different; the national plebiscite system, by excluding Negroes from the basis of representation, would have greatly weakened them.

All this and more became abundantly clear during the debates on section 2 of the Fourteenth Amendment. That section originated in a suggestion made by Professor Francis Lieber of Columbia University.[9] To Lieber and others it seemed outrageous that the effect of the rebellion had been to increase the representation of the Southern states. Prior to the passage of the Thirteenth Amendment they had had nineteen Representatives and Electors for their slave populations and five for free Negroes; now they would have thirteen more—or thirty-seven in all. Since it was plain that the Southern states would not allow the suffrage to persons of African extraction, this increase of representation would redound solely to the advantage of the Southern whites. Lieber therefore suggested that the basis of representation be changed from total population to qualified voters. The effect of the change would be not only to prevent the South from increasing its Negro representation by thirteen but to eliminate that representation altogether. It was soon perceived, however, that Lieber's proposal would work to the disadvantage of some of the other states as well. Throughout the Union various classes of persons, other than Negroes, were excluded from the franchise, though counted in the basis of representation—women and children, unnaturalized foreigners, persons declared disloyal by the several state legislatures, for

[8] *Congressional Globe*, 39th Cong., 1st sess., p. 2939 (Senator Thomas A. Hendricks of Indiana, later Vice President).

[9] *Congressional Globe*, 39th Cong., 1st sess., Appendix, p. 131. See Lieber's *Letter to Hon. E. D. Morgan*, Loyal Publication Society, No. 79 (New York, 1865).

example. But the ratio of these excluded classes to the total population differed widely in the different states. In New England there was a preponderance of women and children; in New York of unnaturalized foreigners; in Missouri, Maryland, West Virginia, and Tennessee of declared rebels. But none of these states wished either to extend the franchise to the excluded classes or to lose the representation on the floor of Congress and in the Electoral College which those classes gave them.

In a famous speech Representative James G. Blaine of Maine demolished the Lieber plan. It would, he said, result in a transfer of power from New England to the West. Taking the census figures of 1860 and equating the number of adult male citizens to the number of qualified voters, he showed that the ratio of voters to population differed very widely in the two sections of the country, varying from a minimum of 19 per cent (in Massachusetts) to a maximum of 58 per cent (in California). The changes which this fact would work in the relative representation of the states would, he declared, be monstrous. California had a population approximately equal to that of Vermont, but it had nearly two and a half times as many voters. Voters being assumed as the basis of apportionment and Vermont being allowed three Representatives, California would be entitled to eight. Indiana, for the same reason, would gain at the expense of Massachusetts. On the basis of population the former was entitled to eleven Representatives and the latter to ten. On the basis of qualified voters, if the former had eleven, the latter would have seven. Was it fair, Blaine asked, that equal masses of people should have unequal representation merely because of the emigration of young voters from the older states to the inviting fields of the Mississippi Valley and the Pacific Slope?

No speech in Congress has ever been more effective. When Blaine was through, the Lieber plan, in its original form, was dead. The Fourteenth Amendment does not rest on the proposition that those whom the states treat as unfit to vote shall not be represented; it was designed only to take away representation from those states in which the right of voting was not given to Negroes; it was so framed as to continue to the Northern and Eastern states their twenty Representatives and Electors based on a non-voting population.

Today several factors have doubtless worked to produce an equality in the ratios of qualified voters to population in the different states: the suffrage amendments to the Constitution; the gradual cessation of the emigration of young voters from the old states to the new; the filling up of the latter by the natural increase of population; and the legal restrictions placed upon immigration from abroad. But the correspondence is still far from exact. Almost any test that could now be devised would produce important disparities. The test of citizenship must work against New York, with its million aliens. A uniform educational test, even if fairly administered throughout the Union, must work against the South with its great numbers of illiterates.

But let it be supposed that the ratio of qualified voters to total population were in fact identical in every state. The national plebiscite system would still not give equal representation to equal masses of population; for in that system representation is based, not on qualified voters, but on actual voters. And different states have different voting habits. Voting is a function of education and economic well-being. It may be stated as a general rule that the ignorant and the depressed classes of society are less likely to exercise the right of suffrage than those that are better off. One might expect therefore that the national plebiscite system would result in a transfer of electoral weight from the worse to the better-educated communities, from the poorer to the richer states.

Voting is also a function of political competition. Close contests bring out the vote. It has long been noticed that states with homogeneous political views produce fewer votes than states of divided sentiments. "Take, for instance," said Representative Aaron H. Cragin in 1866, "the State of Vermont, adjoining New Hampshire. The population of the two States is about the same, but in New Hampshire the contests are always close, and we bring out almost the last vote." [10] In the 1952 elections Maine voted Republican by a majority of 2 to 1; Rhode Island was nearly equally divided between the two parties. But Rhode Island, though the smaller state, cast the greater number of votes.

It would be a useless labor to calculate the intensity and direction of the several forces that would bring about a change in the relative weight of any particular state, were the national plebiscite system to be substituted for the electoral voting system. It is sufficient to notice their composite and final effect. The number of states that would be enfeebled by the change so greatly exceeds the number that would be strengthened that it is perfectly idle to suggest that two thirds of the whole number of states through their Senators and three fourths through their legislatures would consent to it. The vote in the Senate on the Lehman amendment in March, 1957, sufficiently illustrates the point. This was an attempt to substitute the national plebiscite system for a very inferior system recommended by Senators Daniel and Mundt. It was defeated by a vote of 17 yeas to 66 nays. By contrast, the Daniel-Mundt amendment was supported by a vote of 48 to 37—a majority but not two thirds.

[10] *Congressional Globe,* 39th Cong., 1st sess., p. 2943.

When a question is one of power, not argument, it may seem futile to discuss it. Yet, in this case, discussion is not wholly academic. Many genuine reformers in the Senate and House of Representatives have declared that they will vote for no other system than the national plebiscite. Their position is understandable. If the Constitution is amended now in a manner something less than perfect, the day of real reform will be long postponed; for Congress is not likely to act twice on the same matter in a short period of time. It behooves us therefore to look a little more closely at the national plebiscite system, and to ask ourselves whether it is truly as perfect as its sponsors believe it to be. If it is not, some valuable recruits may be gained to the cause of practical reform.

The first point to be noticed has to do with the qualifications of voters. All the amendments proposing the establishment of the national plebiscite system define the electors of the President as "the qualified voters in each state who shall have the qualifications requisite for electors of the most numerous branch of the state legislature." These qualifications, as we have seen, are determined by the laws or constitutions of the several states and are not uniform throughout the Union. Since the weight of a state in the election of the President would, under the national plebiscite system, be directly proportional to the number of voters, it is plain that the establishment of that system would tend to produce an unseemly competition between the states to manufacture new classes of voters. Educational requirements, citizenship requirements, might go by the board. Georgia now permits eighteen-year-olds to vote; other states might be tempted to do likewise, or to reduce the voting age still further, to sixteen, to fifteen, or to fourteen; in 1869, a Congressman from New York proposed, by constitutional amendment, to give the vote to twelve-year-olds; his ideas might again be taken up in some of the states separately.

By the advocates of universal, as contradistinguished from impartial, suffrage, these consequences may be viewed with equanimity. The removal of restrictions upon the suffrage is in itself, they will say, an end devoutly to be wished. But it is very unlikely that such an end would be accomplished throughout the Union. It is much more probable that the measures taken to enlarge the basis of representation in the election of the President would be confined to those states where the suffrage laws are now most liberal. In the states of restricted suffrage, it is likely that the national plebiscite system would produce a contrary effect. Instead of coining new classes of voters they might do away with some classes that already exist; for these states, somewhat oligarchical in tendency, might prefer to withdraw into themselves and abandon the presidential question rather than to enlarge the number of voters. They might, in short, take the ancient posture of South Carolina, which for many years refused to take any effective part in presidential elections, although she remained in the Union, participated in the legislation of Congress, and continued to submit the causes of her citizens to the adjudication of the federal courts.[11]

If these were really the consequences of the national plebiscite system—if some states manufactured classes of voters that other states would refuse to have—great damage might be done to the harmony of the Union. A movement would

[11] See a speech by Mr. Tillman reported in the *South Carolina Legislative Times* for December 7, 1855. This state refused to go into the national conventions and so played no real part in the election. Its lack of interest was strikingly demonstrated in 1836, when it cast its electoral votes for Willie P. Mangum, a man "famous only for his consolidation whiggery and his excessive devotion to his potations."

surely arise to establish by national law a class of federal voters—persons with uniform qualifications entitled to vote for federal officers—the President and Vice President, the Senators and Representatives. And this proposal in turn would be violently opposed. It is one thing to require a uniform mode of voting in the several states and quite another to determine uniform qualifications of the right of suffrage. Rightly or wrongly, the latter has always been held to depend on local peculiarities and so to be appropriately a question for the states themselves to decide.

But let it be assumed that these objections can be got over. The national plebiscite system can be attacked on the ground of principle. The President, we may repeat, is the man of the people and should be chosen according to the sense of the people. The only practical problem that we have to consider is by what means the sense of the people may most accurately be ascertained. No method can be absolutely infallible, but some must be better than others. The national plebiscite system equates the will of the people to the will of the voters; it takes no account whatever of the will of the non-voters, whether these are prevented by law from voting or are silent from choice. The electoral voting system, by contrast, attempts to take into account the will of the non-voters. On the assumption that locality produces a community of interest, that in the administration of national affairs the action of the federal government will redound upon a geographic district to the benefit or detriment of voters and non-voters alike, this system holds that equal masses of population should have equal votes.

The two principles cannot be reconciled. They are based on entirely different ideas of the nature of suffrage. The one holds that a voter votes for himself alone; the other that he votes for the community of which he is a part. According to this second theory, the right to vote is not an individual right to be selfishly exercised, but a social right conferred by the state as a trust to be exercised for others as well as for oneself. Senator Luke P. Poland of Vermont explained the idea very clearly some ninety years ago. "No State or community professing to be republican," said he, "allows all its people to vote. Every one fixes for itself some rule which, in its judgment, will furnish a body of voters or electors who will most wisely and safely represent the wishes and interests of the whole people. . . . The truth is that the whole system of suffrage of any republican State is wholly artificial, founded upon its own ideas of the number and class of persons who will best represent the wishes and interests of the whole people. The right of suffrage is not given to a particular class because they have any greater interest in the Government, or because they have any more natural right to it than others, nor to exercise it for themselves and in their own behalf, but is given to them as fair and proper exponents of the will and interests of the whole community, and to be exercised for the benefit and in the interest of the whole." [12]

It is unnecessary to debate at length the relative merits of these two theories of the suffrage. As long as the right to vote is not unduly restricted by law or compromised in the administration of law, a voting system properly constructed on either theory might be expected to work well. The difference between them lies solely in the position assigned to the non-voting classes. On the principle of one voter, one vote, those who are denied the vote, or who fail to vote, go wholly unrepresented. On the principle of one mass, one vote, they are represented—"constructively" represented—by their immediate neighbors. Which is the better—no repre-

[12] *Congressional Globe*, 39th Cong., 1st sess., p. 2961.

sentation or constructive representation? If the question were merely one of children and parents, aliens and citizens, the uneducated and the educated, there could be little doubt as to the answer. The interests of a community, considered in relation to other communities, are homogeneous. A system that gives unequal weights to equal communities works to the advantage or detriment of everyone within them. An agricultural community usually casts less votes than a manufacturing community of equal numbers; but is that a proper reason for reducing its political weight? Would such a reduction redound to the detriment or benefit of its non-voting population?

The Negro question may, however, be brought in on the other side. In the South it is a notorious fact that very few Negroes vote. Can the Southern Negroes, in any proper sense of the word, be said to be constructively represented by the Southern whites? At first blush the question might seem to answer itself. But the case is not so clear as it appears. If the weight of the South were to be reduced in the determination of national questions, the South as a whole would suffer, but how would that benefit its depressed classes? Would not a general lowering of the economic well-being of the Southern country be more apt to raise than to reduce the temperature of racial antagonism? On the other hand, if the South is permitted to speak with its full voice, the improvement in its economic position may be expected to continue, and that in turn may be expected to lead to an improvement not only in the absolute but also in the relative situation of the Negro population. The difficulties of the Negroes, it must be remembered, are due, not to national laws or to the administration of national laws, but to state laws and *their* administration. Those who have the interests of the Negroes most at heart might be doing them a disservice—they could hardly be doing them any good—by advocating a mode of electing the President which, for a long time to come, must inevitably remove the South from all effective participation in that process.

However this may be, the impossibility of establishing the national plebiscite system by constitutional amendment remains. Not only the Southern states but also the smaller states must oppose it. Any practical scheme of reform must take the electoral voting system as it is and aim at modifying it in such manner as to take the real sense of the people instead of, as at present, the artificial sense of the states.

6. The Proportional Voting System

A second plan of reform, much advocated during the past century, is the proportional voting system. Its idea can best be made clear by an example. New York has 45 electoral votes. Under the general ticket system the presidential candidate who polls the greatest number of popular votes in New York gets all 45 of these electoral votes. Under the proportional voting system each candidate who polled a fraction of the state's popular votes would get the same fraction of its electoral votes. Let it be supposed that A polls four ninths of New York's popular votes, B three ninths, and C two ninths; A, B, and C would be credited with 20, 15, and 10 electoral votes respectively. The national electoral vote for each candidate would be ascertained by adding up the electoral votes that he had won in all the forty-eight states.

This system has three leading features. In the first place, it is a plan of electoral voting. Under it the President would continue to be chosen, or in certain contingencies nominated, by electoral, not popular, votes. In the proposals that have been brought before Congress no change has been suggested either as regards the aggregate number of electoral votes or as regards their distribution among the several states. Out of 531 electoral votes, New York, under the census of 1950, would continue to cast 45, Virginia 12, Nevada 3, and so on. A majority of 266 would still be sufficient for a definitive choice. The number of popular votes cast in any state would have no effect whatever upon its relative weight in the election. South Carolina, for example, would continue to cast her 8 electoral votes, even if only one of her qualified voters went to the polls. In this respect the proportional voting system is the same as the present system. It has the great practical virtue of leaving unchanged the present constitutional formula for determining the relative weight of the states.

In the second place, the proportional voting system would fix the mode of electing the President upon a uniform and permanent principle. It would deprive the state legislatures of the faculty of change. Under the present Constitution a state legislature can, if it wants to, take the appointment of the presidential electors, and consequently the casting of the state's electoral votes, into its own hands; or it can commit this trust to any other person or body of persons of any qualifications whatever. Under the amendments currently being proposed, the casting of a state's electoral votes would be committed by the federal Constitution to the persons having "the qualifications requisite for electors of the most numerous branch of the state legislature." In this regard the proportional voting system would make no change in the practical arrangement that now obtains in the several states separately; for these, acting independently, have given the appointment of the presidential electors to this very description of persons. Nor would it interfere with the existing right of the states to define the qualifications of their own voters in national elections. It would do no more than remove from the state legislatures a power which, in all conscience, they ought not to have.

In the third place—and here is the real point of the proposal—the proportional voting system would recognize the divisions of political sentiment within a state. It would prevent the dominant party from consolidating the state votes and (in effect) counting for itself the popular votes which had been cast against it or not cast at all. It would bring, by the simple processes of arithmetic, the distribution of electoral votes among the several candidates for President into an exactly proportional correspondence with the distribution of popular votes. The system would be operated without the agency of intermediate Electors, and the ratios would be calculated to three decimal places. Earlier schemes of the same type, which retained the agency of the Electors, would have reached approximately the same result by having the Electors chosen in each state by the methods of proportional representation.

The advocates of the proportional voting system justly claim for it all the merits of the national plebiscite system, and they can point in addition to the fact that it stands a very reasonable chance of being adopted. In 1950 the Lodge-Gossett amendment passed the Senate by a vote of 64 to 27, a majority of more than the requisite two thirds. In 1957 an inferior version of this same amendment was supported in the Senate by a smaller majority. These advocates go too far, however, when they pretend that the proportional voting system is, to all intents and purposes, the same as the national plebiscite system; for it can easily be demonstrated that in any reasonably close contest, the two modes of counting may give contrary results. Take two states each having 24 electoral votes and assume that 4,000,000 popular votes are cast in one, 2,400,000 in the other. In state A the Republican receives three fourths of the popular vote, the Democrat one fourth; in state B the Republican receives one eighth, the Democrat seven eighths. The popular vote in the two states together is 3,300,000 for the Republican and 3,100,000 for the Democrat. But under the proportional voting system, the Democrat would be credited with 27 electoral votes to the Republican's 21.

The difference between the two systems can also be shown by applying the formula of proportional voting to the distribution of popular votes actually cast in past elections. In most cases the person who received the greatest number of popular votes in the nation at large would also be found to have received the greatest number of electoral votes. But not in all. In 1880 Garfield obtained more popular votes than Hancock; in 1896 McKinley more than Bryan. The application of the proportional formula would, however, have reversed the order of the candidates.[1]

The point we are making is purely mathematical. We are not saying that Garfield and McKinley would have been elected in 1880 and 1896, respectively, had the national plebiscite system been in effect; nor are we saying that Hancock or Bryan would have been chosen under the proportional voting system. It is impossible to make any pronouncements on this matter. The popular votes in question were not taken under either of these systems but under the general ticket system. That system, with its sure states and doubtful states, with its straight tickets, fusion tickets, and suppressed tickets, imposes a peculiar pattern upon the popular vote. It is certain that under almost any other system of popular voting the

---

[1] See the calculations of Miss Ruth Silva (*Nomination and Election of President and Vice President*, Hearings before a Subcommittee of the Committee on the Judiciary, U.S. Senate, 84th Cong., 1st sess., p. 335).

number of votes cast at any given election would have been greater in the aggregate than it was, and different in the distribution. All we are entitled to say is that in close contests, different modes of counting are liable to produce different results; the proportional voting system will not of necessity produce the same President as the national plebiscite system.

The fact, indeed, has been admitted by the chief proponent of the proportional voting system. Asked by Senator Joseph M. Broughton whether it would be possible under that plan for a man who got a majority of the popular votes not to be elected, Senator Henry Cabot Lodge, Jr., replied: "There is always a theoretical possibility of that happening, so long as you count votes by States, because if you count votes by States the electoral vote attributed to each State remains constant, even if a very small number of citizens come out to vote. The electoral vote in each State can represent therefore a far smaller number of voters in one State than it does in another. . . ." [2]

Let us turn now from exposition to argument. Conceding that the proportional voting system is a reasonably accurate device for taking the sense of the people and much superior for that purpose to the general ticket system, let us ask ourselves whether it ought to be supported as a practicable scheme of reform. To answer this question we must look at the difficulties to which its establishment would immediately or remotely give rise. These I conceive to be three.

Consider first the problem of disputed elections. Under the general ticket system they are practically unknown. That

[2] *Election of President and Vice President*, Hearings before a Subcommittee of the Committee on the Judiciary, U.S. Senate, 81st Cong., 1st sess., p. 6. See also a letter from Senator Henry Cabot Lodge, Jr., in the *New York Times* for January 18, 1949.

is because the system operates in such a way as to make disputes unprofitable. No one would think of demanding a recount of popular votes in a state which had gone one way or the other by a landslide, or in a state where the number of electoral votes involved was too small to affect the order of the candidates in a national election. A very unlikely combination of circumstances would have to occur in order to make a challenge worth while, and even then the dispute would be confined to a few states only. In the past only one election has been disputed. The Hayes-Tilden contest of 1876 stands as an exception out of the rule, and as a warning of the difficulties to which disputed elections lead. Under the proportional voting system such elections would surely be more frequent. The nearly equal division of the two parties in the nation at large would be more accurately represented in the distribution of electoral votes than it is at present. The landslide elections to which we have become accustomed would be replaced by close elections, and close elections would in many cases mean disputed elections. And how would such elections be decided? Is it not apparent that the contest, instead of being confined to one or two doubtful states, would be extended to every state, every county, every election district? For on the principle of ratios a gain anywhere would be a gain everywhere.

Consider next the probable relationship of the President to the majority of the House of Representatives. That body is elected, not by a system of proportional voting, but (mainly) by the district system. In close elections it may therefore happen that a President may be chosen from one party and the majority of the House of Representatives from another. Had the formula for proportional voting been applied to the popular votes actually cast for the presidential candidates in 1880, 1888, and 1896, a Democratic candidate would have been elected contemporaneously with a Republican House of Representatives. From the point of view of legislative and administrative efficiency such a result is not generally to be desired. Sometimes it cannot be avoided. In 1956 any uniform principle of election applied to the choice of the President and the House of Representatives would surely have brought in General Eisenhower with a Democratic House. But it does not seem the part of wisdom to take the sense of the people according to one principle in choosing the President and according to another in choosing the House of Representatives. The accidents of arithmetic alone may cause the people to speak with two different voices at the same time.

The main objection to the proportional voting system is, however, one of principle. The underlying idea of that system is that equal ideological masses of people, rather than equal geographical masses, are entitled to equal votes; and that, I submit, is an idea that ought not to be introduced into our institutions. The difficulty here stems, not from the application of this principle to the distribution of the electoral votes, for these are not sentient beings, but from the danger that the same principle will be extended to the representation of the states in Congress.

The connection between electoral voting and representation in Congress is very close. The electoral body has often been likened to Congress in joint convention.[3] Senator Abraham Baldwin of Georgia, who had been a member of the Federal Convention, once remarked that the Electors were a constitutional branch of the government as respectable as Congress, and in whom the Constitution in the business of

---

[3] E.g., 33 *Annals*, 142 (Mahlon Dickerson [1819]).

electing a President had more confidence than in Congress.[4] Many of the early amendments proposing the establishment of a uniform mode of appointing Electors by the people in districts suggested the same mode for choosing Representatives. Many of the plans introduced in the 1870's, similar in principle to Senator Lodge's, but retaining the Electors, would have worked equally well for Representatives; Senator Lodge's own plan could be adapted to Representatives by giving the odd congressional seats remaining after each party's integral quota had been filled to the parties having the largest fractions. If we admit the principle of P.R.—the proportional representation of ideological groups—in the distribution of a state's electoral votes, it will be hard to deny it in the distribution of a state's congressional seats. And P.R. in Congress, as we shall presently demonstrate, would be an unqualified evil.

But is the proportional voting system really based on the principle of P.R.? The allegation has frequently been denied, and by no one more firmly than by Senator Lodge. "The proposed constitutional amendment," he said in a letter to the press, "has no relation whatever to 'proportional representation.' It could not have. . . . Proportional representation cannot be applied to the election of a single official. It is impossible to take one man and divide him up proportionately— or otherwise—and expect him to live." [5] This, however, is not answering to the point. It has never been suggested that the proportional voting system would divide up the President proportionately or otherwise; but would it not divide, according to the principle of P.R., the whole number of electoral votes allocated to each state? In 1912 New York's rep-

---

[4] 10 *Annals*, 30.
[5] *New York Herald Tribune*, March 23, 1950.

resentation in the Electoral College consisted of forty-five members, all of whom voted for Wilson. Had these been chosen by the system of proportional representation, 19 votes would have been cast for Wilson, 13 for Taft, 11 for Roosevelt, and 2 for Debs. The Lodge-Gossett amendment, being based on the same formula, would, to the nearest whole numbers, have produced the same result. The mere fact that this amendment, by abolishing the agency of the intermediate Electors, requires no machinery for translating fractions into integers cannot be held to affect its underlying principle. Messrs. Hoag and Hallett of the Proportional Representation League made the point very clearly in their book *Proportional Representation*. Under the caption "How P.R. should be applied to the Presidency," they wrote: "Obviously we cannot have proportional representation in the Presidency because it is a single office, but we can have it in the electoral college or in the distribution of electoral votes." [6] The proportional voting system, as advocated by Senator Lodge, has it in the distribution of electoral votes.

We may add that the principle of the proportional voting system has been identified for many years with the principle of P.R. If we trace the proportional features of the Lodge-Gossett amendment backward through history, we come eventually to the Maish amendment of 1877. This amendment was described by one of its sponsors (Senator Buckalew) in the *North American Review* for March, 1877, under three heads of remark: "First, it provides for a direct vote by the people for President and Vice President; second, it retains electoral votes as at present, while dispensing with electors and electoral colleges; and third, it assigns to candidates elec-

[6] C. H. Hoag and G. H. Hallett, *Proportional Representation* (New York, 1926), p. 320.

toral votes from each State in proportion to popular votes received by them therein." [7]

The only difference between the Maish proposal and the Lodge proposal is that Maish would have awarded the votes represented by the sum of the decimals to the candidates having the largest fractions—that is to say, he would have made an integral distribution of the electoral votes. In the same year an exact counterpart of the Lodge proposal, even to the three places of decimals, was contained in an amendment introduced by Representative Cravens. In 1878 a similar proposal was reported by a committee of the House of Representatives.

The Maish amendment was described by J. Hampden Dougherty in his book *The Electoral System* as "embodying some of the principles of the Hare plan for minority representation." [8] H. V. Ames, in his *Proposed Amendments to the Constitution*, praises this same amendment as an "application of the system of proportional representation to the election of President and Vice President." [9]

But let us come down to more recent times. The immediate predecessor of the Lodge-Gossett amendment was the Lea-Walsh amendment of 1928 and subsequent years. The Lea amendment was endorsed time and again by the Proportional Representation League as an application of P.R. to presidential elections. Nor was Senator Walsh reticent as to its true nature. Pending a change in the Constitution of the United States, he called upon the states to adopt P.R. in the Electoral Colleges of their own volition. On May 29, 1928, he introduced Senate Concurrent Resolution 32, which read in part as follows: "Whereas proportional representation . . . has

[7] 124 *North American Review*, p. 170.
[8] P. 351. Thomas Hare was the inventor of the system of proportional, or minority, representation popularized by J. S. Mill.
[9] P. 98.

proved to be easily workable, satisfactory to the voters, and just to all parties . . . Resolved . . . that the legislatures of the several States should establish by appropriate legislation proportional representation in the choosing of presidential electors." [10]

Finally, we may notice the view taken of the Lodge-Gossett amendment itself by the present-day advocates of P.R. In the department called "Proportional Representation" of the *National Municipal Review* for June, 1948, the progress of the Lodge and Gossett resolutions in Congress is reported under the caption, "P.R. for Presidential Electoral Votes Advances."

Leaving this barren question of terminology with the observation that when two things are exactly the same, it is well to call them by the same name, let us turn to a more interesting topic. Would the application of the principle of P.R. to the distribution of the presidential electoral votes be harmful to our institutions? If we keep our eyes firmly fixed on the presidential contest and refuse to look at the possibility that the principle of P.R. may come to be extended, by imitation, from the distribution of electoral votes to the distribution of seats in Congress, we must probably answer this question in the negative.

The system of P.R., when applied to a deliberative assembly, works badly because it promotes the multiplication of political parties, fills the assembly with unfit characters, and establishes the relationship between the representative and his constituency upon an improper base. But an aggregation of electoral votes is not a deliberative assembly. A group of persons having a common object, if it can gain a seat or two in Congress, has every incentive to establish and maintain

[10] Senator Magnus Johnson of Minnesota had made the same suggestion February 17, 1925.

itself as a distinct political entity; for a seat in Congress is a valuable property, and he who occupies it can advance the interests of his constituents in a variety of ways and for a considerable period of time. But it is difficult to see what advantage could accrue to a minor party from the privilege of translating its popular votes by a mathematical formula into electoral votes; for the efficacy of those votes would generally be nil. Without the agency of intermediate Electors they could not be used to change the order of the leading candidates; only occasionally might they serve to throw the election of the President into the House of Representatives. The mere opportunity of casting a few electoral votes for a candidate who is beaten in advance can hardly be expected to prevent a minor party from withering and dying in the ordinary course.

Nor can objections to the system of P.R. based on the kind of men that it tends to select or on their relationships to their constituencies have any meaning when that system is applied to electoral votes. The functions of men in a deliberative assembly are to argue, to compromise, and to decide; the function of an electoral vote is to be counted, without discretion, for a predetermined person.

It has been necessary to make these observations because the nature of the theoretical objection to the proportional voting system has been widely misunderstood and misrepresented. The danger is not that P.R. in the presidential contest will bring about a proliferation of parties on the French model but that P.R. will be extended to the House of Representatives. This danger I conceive to be real. Let it be assumed that the Lodge-Gossett amendment or something like it is adopted and that the system of proportion is applied throughout the nation to the presidential election. Would that event advance the cause of those who would apply the same system to a state's representation in Congress? It seems probable that it would. In the first place, the new system would provide a precedent, and, as the late Senator Homer Ferguson once remarked, no one needs to be told the importance of precedent in democratic government. In the second place, it would popularize the principle of proportional representation by exhibiting its mathematical advantages and concealing its political defects. In the third place, it would almost compel those whose votes had brought it about to support the extension of its principle in other directions; they would find it difficult to explain to a vigorous minority why it was entitled to a proportion of a state's electoral votes but not to a proportion of the same state's representation in the House.

The establishment of proportional representation in the congressional delegations might come about in one of two ways. It might be introduced piecemeal by the legislatures of the several states. Section 3 of the Apportionment Act of 1911, prescribing that Representatives shall be elected on the single-member district system, is no longer on the statute books. It was declared by the Supreme Court in 1932 to have expired by its own limitation with the apportionment to which it related.[11] Congress has never re-enacted the provision.

Proportional representation might also be introduced in the House of Representatives by Congress itself. Suppose that the general ticket system should come to be established by the state legislatures as the ordinary mode of choosing representatives—that is to say, if Congressmen should come to be elected at large rather than in districts. The evils consequent upon the change would soon give rise to a movement for reform. Congress would be called upon to exercise its original and

[11] Wood *v.* Brown, 287 U.S. 1.

concurrent power to make or alter the state regulations respecting the manner of holding elections for Representatives. It would have a choice of remedies. It might do what it did in 1842, when it was faced with a similar difficulty: It might require the states to choose their Representatives in single-member districts. But with the example of the Lodge-Gossett amendment before it, it might plump for the system of proportional representation. The contingency is not so remote as it might seem. Some states now use the general ticket system to choose Representatives; others have experimented with it from time to time. In 1932 the invalidation of Virginia's redistricting law caused that state to elect all its Representatives at large. The Virginia Democrats had previously conceded the election of one Republican under the district method, but when the votes were counted by the general ticket mode, a solid Democratic delegation was found to have been elected. Shortly afterwards an acute writer remarked: "It is conceivable that increased prevalence . . . of such situations resulting from election of representatives at large, will increase the demand for proportional representation." [12]

To complete the chain of the argument it only remains to show that the scheme of proportional representation, if applied to Congress, would be inconsistent with the conditions prerequisite to the successful operation of congressional government. These prerequisites I conceive to be two. First, the mass of Congress must be composed of moderate men. A Congress made up of immoderate men—persons unwilling to compromise but eager to press the tenets of their party to impossible conclusions—could not legislate at all. Second, the constituencies of Congress must leave it alone. A Congress

[12] Hubert Searcy, "Congressional Redistricting in the Solid South," *Birmingham-Southern College Bulletin* (May, 1936), p. 37.

controlled by its constituencies, with no other function than to collect and examine its instructions, would not be a governing but a registering body. Bagehot, when the idea of proportional representation was still young, remarked that "constituency government is the precise opposite of parliamentary government. It is the government of immoderate persons far from the scene of action, instead of the government of moderate persons close to the scene of action." [13] But long before Bagehot, Representative Thomas Hartley of Pennsylvania, a member of the First Congress, had expressed the same views: "I apprehend, sir, that Congress will be the best judges of proper measures, and that instructions will never be resorted to but for party purposes, when they will generally contain the prejudices and acrimony of the party, rather than the dictates of honest reason and sound policy." [14]

Now, I submit, that one of the very best ways to secure a moderate man in Congress is to take him from a geographic constituency, and one of the very worst ways is to take him from what Bagehot called a voluntary constituency. The great majority of men in a geographic constituency wear their party principles lightly: They are distrustful of zealots and scornful of party hacks; when they choose a candidate, or when a candidate is presented to them by the local boss, that person is likely to be a person of middle-of-the-road views and a certain independence of party dictation.

It would be otherwise with voluntary constituencies. Most of these would of course return members for the great parties. But since their unity would be mathematical rather than local, they would play no real part in the selection of their

[13] Walter Bagehot, *The English Constitution* (New York, 1877), p. 214.
[14] 1 *Annals of Congress*, 732-733.

representatives; indeed, it would be hard to say what voters were in what constituency and to what constituency any particular member owed his election. Everything would be controlled by the party managers, from the manufacture of the constituencies to the selection of the candidates. And what the party managers would look for in their members would be obedience, not thought.

But there would be many voluntary constituencies besides those of the great parties. Every group of persons in the country with a strong common interest would go about the business of making up a constituency; and the members for these constituencies would be zealous men, characteristic of their parties and therefore immoderate.

The relationship of Congress to its constituencies must likewise be very different under the two plans. A geographic constituency, except when the passions of the people are excited, will ordinarily leave its representatives alone. A voluntary constituency will almost always hold them to party violence. The reason has been well explained: "At present the member is free because the constituency is not in earnest: no constituency has an acute, accurate doctrinal creed in politics. The law made the constituencies by geographical divisions; and they are not bound together by close unity of belief. They have vague preferences for particular doctrines and that is all. But a voluntary constituency would be a church with tenets; it would make its representative the messenger of its mandates, and the delegate of its determinations." [15]

In conclusion, we must say that the chief question to answer with respect to any amendment proposing that the President be chosen by the proportional voting system is whether its adoption would or would not facilitate the intro-

[15] Bagehot, *English Constitution*, p. 224.

duction of proportional representation in Congress. If it would not, then it might well be supported as a distinct improvement on the general ticket system. If it would, or even if it might, then every effort should be made to defeat it or, better still, to exchange it for an amendment of a sounder type.

7. The Single-Member District System

In recent years a third plan of reform has been revived. This is the single-member district system—the mode which, according to Madison, "was mostly, if not exclusively, in view when the Constitution was framed and adopted." [1] Its leading idea is that, in ascertaining the degree of public confidence bestowed upon the several candidates for President at the November election, the sense of the people should be taken by districts instead of by states. Under the general ticket system the candidates are arranged in order of popularity by a formula which disregards differences of sentiment within states. Under the district system these differences of sentiments, which must almost necessarily exist, at least in the larger states, would be taken into account. For the rest the two systems are the same. Both are based on the proposition that the representation of constituencies in the Electoral College, [2] as in the House of Representatives, should be related to

[1] Madison to George Hay, August 23, 1823 (Madison, *Writings*, IX, 151-152).

[2] For convenience of exposition I shall assume in this chapter that the people continue to cast their electoral votes through the agency

numbers of inhabitants rather than to numbers of potential voters or of votes cast. Both use geographical rather than ideological constituencies. Both qualify the right of suffrage by the same rules which the states have severally prescribed for the choice of Representatives in Congress. Both are plurality systems—that is to say, they give the electoral votes of their several constituencies to the candidates obtaining the greatest number of popular votes within them, whether or not that number is an absolute majority of the votes cast. The only but the great substantive difference between them is that one gives the President a federative, the other a national, origin.

If the United States were a single political unit, the machinery for working the district system would be very easy. At each census the country would be divided into five hundred and thirty-one electoral districts, in each of which the number of inhabitants should be the same; and these districts would be the only constituencies and elect the President. But the case is more difficult. The connection between the forty-eight states is federal; and by the terms of the compact their relative weights in the election of the President are fixed by a formula in which the principle of numbers is modified by the principle of state equality. The number of Electors allocated to each state by the Constitution is compounded of the number of its Representatives and the number of its Senators in the national legislature; Representatives are apportioned among the several states by a federal rule founded on the aggregate numbers of their inhabitants;[3] Senators are

---

of intermediate Electors. If they were to cast these votes directly for the presidential candidates, the district system might operate more simply, but it would suffer no change of principle.

[3] Nevada is an exception. Not entitled to a Representative on the score of numbers, she has one by the rule that "each state shall have at least one Representative."

not. Assuming, as we probably must, that a constitutional majority could not be found either in the Senate or in the state legislatures for an amendment that would abolish the ninety-six Electors corresponding to the ninety-six Senators, we are faced at the outset by a dilemma which, to those who found their political calculations on arithmetical principles alone, may seem very perplexing. How can the present formula for distributing Electors be maintained and the country as a whole still be divided into equal districts? If the number of districts in each state is equated to the whole number of its Electors, the districts will not be equal in different states; the greater states must support larger constituencies than the smaller ones. If the number of districts in each state is equated to the number of its Representatives in Congress, to the exclusion of its Senators, the districts will be equal in the several states, but they cannot be the only constituencies; 96 electoral votes—two per state—will remain to be cast by a different arrangement of voters.

There is no breaking the horns of this dilemma; still we may cast them off with the observation that an inability to elect the President by the best possible system cannot be alleged as a reason for not electing him by the best system possible. The only real problem is to decide on one method or another of fitting the 96 extra votes into the district scheme. As a matter of fact this decision would appear already to have been taken. All modern district system amendments are founded on the principles of what used to be called the New Jersey Plan—in deference to Senator Dickerson of that state, who repeatedly brought it forward during the second and third decades of the last century. This plan would relate the number of electoral districts in each state to the number of its Representatives in Congress, leaving the two Electors corresponding to its Senators to be chosen by the people of the state, voting at large. New York, for example, would be divided into forty-three equal districts; the people of each of these districts, through their qualified voters would, in effect, cast one vote for President; in addition, the people of the state as a whole would cast two votes.

The fault of this scheme, judged by the stated principles of the district system, is immediately apparent. It is conceivable that the distribution of the 96 state votes among the several candidates might be such as to reverse the order of the leaders in the district voting. By hypothesis, a candidate with 218 out of 435 district votes is the favorite of the people at large, but unless he can garner half the state votes, his ultimate election cannot be certain; he may even be defeated in the Electoral College. But this is an unavoidable fault. It is the consequence, not of the New Jersey Plan, but of the federal compromise. Unless we are prepared and able to change that compromise—to implement the suggestion made in 1819 by Senator James Barbour and Representative Henry St. George Tucker, both of Virginia, that the number of Electors be apportioned to the number of Representatives alone instead of to the number of Representatives and Senators combined [4]—we must accept the risk that the will of the people may, upon occasion, be defeated by the will of the states. We may comfort ourselves with the reflection that such occasions must be rare and that when they occur, the voice of the people must necessarily have been indistinct. It is impossible that a candidate clearly favored by the district constituencies should be defeated by the state constituencies, for the voters in both sets of constituencies are the same persons, and the number of district votes vastly exceeds the number of state votes.

As compared with other forms of the district system, the

[4] 33 *Annals*, 164; 34 *Annals*, 1420.

New Jersey Plan has the merit of convenience; it obviates the necessity that a state might otherwise be under of forming two sets of districts—one for the choice of Representatives and the other, a little more numerous, for the casting of electoral votes. It has also the merit of bringing into a clear view the underlying principle of the district system—that equal masses of persons should have equal representation—and of exhibiting the modification of that principle by the principle of state equality, a modification necessitated by the federal compromise. Finally, it has the merit of providing the states with a fairly constructed arrangement of districts, susceptible of being used for the election of Representatives as well as for the casting of electoral votes; as we shall presently insist, the mere existence of these districts must tend to prevent the states from choosing their Representatives, as some of them now do, in whole or in part by the general ticket or the gerrymandering system.

The arguments in favor of establishing by constitutional amendment a uniform mode of electing the President by districts have been adverted to, at least by implication, in some of the earlier chapters of this book. It may be useful to summarize them here. One concession, however, the reader must be prepared to make to the expositor. He must take it for granted that the injunctions of the Constitution respecting the establishment of districts will be faithfully followed by those to whom they are addressed. If he insists on assuming that the district boundaries will not be fairly drawn, or that some districts will choose more than the Elector, or that more than two Electors per state will be chosen at large, he can never understand, let alone answer, the questions at issue. It will be time enough to say that the principles of the district system cannot be reduced to practice when the proponents of that system have proved its theoretical desirability.

As with most other proposals for reform, a district system amendment would place the mode of electing the President out of the control of the forty-eight state legislatures and give to it the stability and uniformity that are essentially involved in the elementary notion of a constitutional regulation. In this connection we must never forget that, under the present Constitution, the separate state legislatures possess the faculty of change. Nor must we suppose that they will never exercise it. "All experience proves," said a very experienced politician, "that it is in the nature of political parties to 'feel power and forget right.' The end which every party proposes to itself, as the object of its united effort, is power. In the pursuit of this object, the majority lose that sense of justice which should protect the rights of the weaker party. They easily persuade themselves that the good of the country will be promoted by excluding their opponents from power, and, under the delusive belief that they are sustained by patriotic motives, they commit the most flagrant acts of outrage upon the minority." [5] What is the history of the establishment of the general ticket system for the appointment of presidential Electors, or of the general ticket and gerrymandering systems for the election of Representatives, but a long illustration of the truth of these propositions? It is not merely for the sake of constitutional symmetry that steadiness and uniformity in the mode of electing the President should be secured by the Constitution itself. They are indispensable to the existence of that political justice which has been called the bond and cement of our Union.

The next great advantage of the district system—and this too it shares with other plans of reform—is that it would make the President in fact, what he is in theory, the man

[5] II *Register of Debates*, 1367-1368 (George McDuffie).

of the people. It would put it out of the power of the great states, or of the dominant parties in the great states, to consolidate their votes in such a way as to override the dominant party in the country at large. If the President is to be elected by electoral votes, it seems plain that every equal mass of persons entitled by the Constitution to be represented by one vote should also be entitled to cast that vote for the candidate of its own choice. A system that permits the minority votes in each state to be counted for the majority cannot be fair and must sometimes, if not frequently, result in the defeat of the popular candidate.

That the district system would reduce the effect of fraud and accident in the election of the President is a judgment that will hardly be disputed. Under the general ticket system small and local causes can produce great and comprehensive results. A few popular votes in a single district of New York, counted erroneously or cast for some occasional reason, can produce a transfer of 45 electoral votes from one candidate to another—a swing of 90 votes as between these two. Under the district system the same circumstance could produce, in any state, a transfer of but 3 electoral votes—the district vote and the two state-wide votes—or a swing of 6.

The district system would also make it impossible for minor parties and pressure groups in the so-called doubtful states to defeat, for their own ends, the will of the people at large. This is a point upon which it is necessary to have clear ideas. No one can deny the right of a third party to act as arbiter between the two major parties upon occasions when neither of them commands an absolute majority of the suffrages of the people. This right is an adjunct of the right to vote. No party is obligated to put up a candidate of its own and, in effect, to throw away its votes in a hopeless cause. Every party, every combination of individuals, every separate person, has a right to make an opinion felt, even if only in choosing what they, or he, may consider the lesser of two evils. No one can say that the admission of this right amounts to a surrender of the election to a minor party. If, in choosing the President, the balance of power should be held by the Communist party or by a communion of saints, the case would be the same. Neither could elect a President of its own; they could but choose which of the two major parties should make one. But the right of arbitration does not extend to cases in which there is nothing in dispute. If a majority of the people favor the election of a Democrat as President, neither the Communists nor the saints have a right to put in a Republican. One of the great evils of the general ticket system is that it permits a minor party, especially in one of the great doubtful states, to defeat the clearly expressed will of the people in the nation at large. For purposes of illustration let it be supposed that a candidate comes to New York with 265 electoral votes to his opponent's 221, and let it further be supposed that, in spite of the general ticket, this ratio truly reflects the relative strength of the candidates in the country outside of New York. In New York, however, the candidates are equally matched, and the balance of power is held by a minor group. Is it not apparent that, by giving the 45 votes of New York to the candidate of the national minority, this minor group can defeat the will of the majority? The district system would operate differently. It would give the balance of power to a minor party only when the major parties were evenly matched in the country at large. And that, I submit, is as it should be.

The opinions of Madison and others that political parties would be less sectional under the district system than under the general ticket system have been quoted in another place. And indeed it is clear that where each single district in the country as a whole gives a distinct vote, the political character of the votes will not so probably be identified by geographical sections, but will be more interspersed through all sections of the country. The Southern states are predominantly Democratic, but they are not so solidly Democratic as they appear to be in the electoral vote. It cannot be doubted that under a fairly constructed system of districts, they would cast a number of Republican votes. Under the general ticket system, as it ordinarily operates in the so-called safe states, no condition of the country, no conduct of the government, produces the least apparent change in their political complexion. Under the district system, national considerations would affect the distribution of their votes and permit them to play a national, rather than a sectional, role in the election of the President.

Finally, the district system would compel the two major parties to look for their candidates in the country at large rather than in the great states alone. In the party conventions, and subsequently in the presidential election, the question would be, not who is the man of New York, California, Pennsylvania, Illinois, and Ohio, but who is the man of the nation.

This is a formidable list of advantages, difficult to be dealt with by the defenders of the general ticket system or the advocates of other plans. Nevertheless, whenever a district system amendment has been proposed, a variety of objections have been taken to it. They may be classified under three heads: those that are grounded on the sacred character of the Constitution and the danger of rash amendments; those addressed to the pride and jealousy of the states; and those which result from a comparison of the district system with the general ticket system, the proportional voting system, or the national plebiscite system.

There has always been a class of persons who, in their undiscriminating reverence for the excellencies and imperfections of the Constitution, have been disposed to regard every proposition to amend it as a dangerous innovation. "I would sooner lay down my hand, and have it cut off," said Edward Everett of Massachusetts, "than hold it up in favor of alteration." [6] "The ground on which we tread is sacred," said another; "the Convention who framed the Constitution seemed to have been inspired in their labours." [7] Arguments of this type, more suitable to priests than statesmen, can with difficulty be met to the satisfaction of those who make them. A partial answer, however, was returned by Representative McDuffie in 1826: "Although it is undoubtedly true, that every change is not an improvement, and that the Constitution ought never to be altered, even under the clearest convictions of theoretical propriety, for 'slight or transient' causes, yet it is equally true, that to stand indiscriminately opposed to all changes, is, to say the least of it, the dictate of a very superficial wisdom. It is offering an idolatrous homage at the shrine of the Constitution, which the Constitution itself explicitly disclaims. That the clause which provides for its own amendment, stands amongst the least equivocal indications of the wisdom of its framers, will be apparent to every one who will reflect but for a single moment, upon the vast comprehensiveness of their labors, and the peculiar circumstances under which they were performed." [8]

That McDuffie's answer is not a complete justification of a district system amendment is obvious. It goes only to open the subject to debate and to define the party upon whom lies the burden of proof. Conceding that it is unwise frequently to change the fundamental principles of government,

[6] II *Register of Debates*, 1711; cf. *ibid.*, 1573 (1826).
[7] II *Register of Debates*, 1863; cf. *ibid.*, 1398 (Henry R. Storrs).
[8] II *Register of Debates*, 1366 (1826).

conceding also that the Constitution of the United States is peculiar in its structure and should be altered only in cases of imperious necessity, it merely insists that the advocates of the district system be permitted to establish the affirmative of their proposition, or at least to make the attempt. Two lines of argument are open to them. In the first place, they can deny that a district system amendment would in fact change the fundamental principles of government. "This plan," said Senator Dickerson in 1819, "of dividing the States into districts, is no new experiment; it is no innovation, whatever, upon the Constitution; it is only calculated to render permanent and uniform a regulation which has prevailed in nearly all the States, and which ought to have prevailed in all, and would have prevailed in all, by common consent, but for the disorganizing spirit of party." [9] Some years earlier Representative William Gaston of North Carolina had made the same point: "When we come to examine the Constitution, and compare it with the proposed amendment, we shall find that the object is not to introduce new, but to invigorate old principles: to give a practical operation to the instrument which consists with its designed effect—to rescue it from perversion and abuse." [10] In the second place, advocates of the district system can admit, for purposes of argument, that the establishment of a uniform mode of electing the President by the people in districts would change the principles of the Constitution by excluding other modes; then they must assert the necessity of the change. The advantages to be expected from the district system have been explained above; whether they are sufficient to warrant a constitutional amendment is the question to be decided by those authorized to make such amendments. All that we need say here is that reverence for

[9] 33 *Annals*, 139 (1819).
[10] 26 *Annals*, 837 (1814).

the Constitution, laudable as it may be, does not relieve those who oppose change, merely because it *is* change, from the necessity of listening to the arguments for alteration, nor justify them in stubbornly and stupidly refusing an amendment that time and experience have shown to be necessary.

Equally illogical, and for that reason equally difficult to deal with, are the objections to the district system addressed to state pride. An example will clarify their nature. New York, it is said, is a great state; under the general ticket system it casts 45 votes for President, but let the district system be established and its importance may dwindle down to a solitary vote; even Nevada may defeat it. Or look at Missouri. In 1956 it cast 13 votes for Stevenson; but so evenly was the state divided in its political sentiments that under the New Jersey district plan, its net weight in the election might have been one vote; and that vote might have been cast for either candidate, depending on the manner in which the district boundaries were drawn.

The error in this argument is very gross. The weight of a state in the Electoral College depends solely on the number of its seats in that body, and not on the distribution of those seats between political parties. "Virginia, voting by Districts, is Virginia still—divested of none of her attributes, as a separate member of the confederacy. . . . Each State will give precisely the same number of electoral votes for President that she is now entitled to give, under the existing provisions of the Constitution." [11] Such was McDuffie's reply to the suggestion that the weight of a state would be reduced if its sentiments were truly reflected in the Electoral College. Further to demonstrate the fallacy, let us assume that the legislature of New York were to extend, as it has the constitutional power to

[11] II *Register of Debates*, 1375-1376 (1826).

extend, the general ticket system from the appointment of Electors to the election of Representatives. All New York's Republican members or all its Democratic members, as the case might be, would be turned out of Congress; but would any man pretend that New York would be more correctly represented, or approve the act? We cannot presume it. The case of the President is the same. His election is not a state but a national question. Where a state is divided in its votes, it stands neutral, and no man can say that it ought not to. But its weight in the election remains the same, however that weight may be distributed in the electoral scales.

Another argument has been addressed to the states in their corporate capacities. We have been told that the establishment of the district system will destroy state rights. Senator John F. Kennedy of Massachusetts, in a recent defense of the present plan of the Constitution, put the matter very briefly: "We are no longer treating each State as a sovereign unit which decides how its votes shall be cast. We are nationalizing the states in one particular. . . . I regard it as a step backward." [12]

In considering the validity of this argument we must keep in mind the question upon which it turns. The comparison is not between the district system and the general ticket system but between the district system and the subsisting plan of the Constitution, in other words, as a Congressman on the same side as Senator Kennedy once expressed it, [13] between the district system and the faculty of violent and arbitrary change, from one system to another, on the part of the state legislatures.

Let it be conceded, say those who would preserve the faculty of change, that the district system is the best system;

[12] 102 *Congressional Record*, 5336.
[13] II *Register of Debates*, 1448 (William S. Archer of Virginia).

let it even be supposed that it has been admitted by uniform adoption; it would still be improper to give it the permanence of a constitutional regulation. Control over the mode of the election of the President has been given for wise purposes to the state legislatures as an instrument of efficient and salutary action on the administration of the general government. Let a district system, indeed any system, be once fixed and made unalterable, and this control is at an end. If a district system be recognized, either by convenience or opinion, it is in the competency of the states, by the present plan of the Constitution, to adopt it. But the main faculty of their control on the administration of the general government consists in the power of departure from this system as exigency requires. Every state must be enabled to throw a collected and decisive impetus on the unadjusted and vacillating lever of the election of a President. A state may diffuse and spread out the members of its power in relaxation, but no manacle must prevent its collecting and drawing up this strength when the season of efficient action impends and the blow for public safety is required to be struck.

Such are the arguments that have been made over the years by the defenders of the faculty of change. It is easy to show that they are totally without merit. Let it be assumed that the people of the United States do in fact, by constitutional amendment, establish a uniform system of voting by districts for President. In form, such an amendment would certainly abridge the power of the state legislatures, for it would narrow their discretion as to the manner of appointing Electors. But would it deprive them of any beneficial power, any power which they could exercise otherwise than abusively? It will not be pretended that there is anything in the local situation of the several states that renders differences in the mode of appointing Electors desirable; it has been repeatedly admitted that uniformity of movement in the state legislatures is greatly to be wished in this respect. What conceivable object could a state legislature have in wanting to preserve the faculty of change? In exercising it, what could it hope to accomplish? The answer is plain: By changing on the eve of an election from the district system to the general ticket system, by counting for the state majority, district votes which had been cast for the state minority, it might succeed in bringing in its own candidate for President ahead of the candidate of the nation. But what depending crisis or occasion could justify such a proceeding? None can be imagined. The large states—and it is the large states only that gain by a system of consolidated voting—have no legitimate claim to substitute their will for the will of the nation.

Many years ago a Representative from New York, Jabez D. Hammond, now remembered chiefly as the political historian of his state, made the point very clear: "Sir, the question of who shall be elected President is not a State, but a national question. The President is an officer who exists for the benefit of the people of the United States, and not for any one State or any part of the States. He ought not, therefore, to be created by the States but by the people. . . . A great State cannot claim, because she is great, that she should furnish a Chief Magistrate for the nation." [14]

Hammond was speaking at a time when the faculty of change was being exercised by the state legislatures at every election. He was exposing the error or the insincerity of those who pretended that consolidated voting is the "extreme medicine" of the state. Now that the extreme medicine of the state has become its daily bread, do the arguments against the faculty of change hold any less water? One cannot

[14] 30 *Annals*, 309 (1816).

think so. It is difficult to imagine the case in which a change of mode upon the part of a state legislature could be imputed to proper motives. A shift from the general ticket to the district system would relax rather than draw up state power; it would benefit only the state minority; the motives for such a shift could only be those which actuated the Michigan legislature in 1892. A shift from the general ticket system to the mode of legislative election, such as that made by Florida in 1868, could be explained only as a device for defeating the will of the state majority by refining it through a system of districts gerrymandered for the election of the state legislature.

It is a curious fact that the persons best known to history as the defenders of state rights—Jefferson, Madison, Macon, and others—have never included among those rights the faculty of changing the mode of electing the President. "Sir," said McDuffie of South Carolina upon one occasion, "it cannot be disguised, that this idea of infringing the rights of the States, by fixing a uniform system of popular suffrage, is founded upon the latent delusion that the *Legislatures* of the States have rights, paramount to those of the *People* of the States. And this I pronounce an arrant heresy." [15] James K. Polk, another staunch protector of state rights, backed up McDuffie in the same debate: "Does the plan of amendment proposed, take from the large States any of their rights? No; on the contrary, it gives to the People of every portion of such States, the power of being heard and felt in the election. It takes from their servants in the Legislature, it is true, the power of suppressing the voice of the minority in the State by the operation of the general ticket system, or by the election of Electors by the Legislature; but it gives the power which it thus takes from their servants, which may be, and

[15] II *Register of Debates*, 1943 (1826).

is often abused, not to the Federal Government but to the People of those States themselves." [16]

These considerations suggest that state rights have nothing to do with the district system amendment. That amendment would not abridge the just rights of any State but would add to the security of all. It would take away from the state legislatures only a matter of detail and regulation, onerous in itself, furnishing the materials for factious intrigue and maneuver, and productive of no advantage to the people of the states.

It is remarkable that Senator Kennedy, at the same time that he was defending the faculty of change as a state right, should have proposed an amendment to the Constitution requiring the election of the President to be made by a uniform general ticket system.[17]

The opponents of a district system amendment to the Constitution sometimes argue from grounds of convenience and expediency. What, they ask, is the principal objection to the general ticket system? Is it not that the votes of the minority in each state are impressed into the service of the majority? And would not the case be the same under the district system? A district would contain nearly 350,000 inhabitants; its political sentiments might be homogeneous or divided; but in either case it would cast its single electoral vote for the candidate of the plurality party. What difference does it make whether the votes of minorities are impressed by districts or by states? If impressment is wrong, where is the remedy, if we exchange the general ticket for the district system? If impressment is right or unavoidable, does it make much difference whether the vote is taken in forty-eight districts or in five hundred and thirty-one? If we are not prepared, or not able, to adopt the national plebiscite or the pro-

[16] II *Register of Debates*, 1651.
[17] 102 *Congressional Record*, 5574.

portional voting system, we might as well play along with the general ticket system. Jefferson made the argument in 1800; [18] Edward Everett in 1826; [19] Senators Paul H. Douglas and John F. Kennedy today.[20]

The reasoning, however, is fallacious. It would have some validity if the forty-eight states were of equal size and had equal numbers of electoral votes. But even then it would not prove that there is no practical difference between the general ticket and the district systems. Both are grounded on what might be called the theory of compensation. Recognizing that there may, indeed, be a considerable difference between the relative strength of the minorities in any two districts, the advocates of both systems suggest, upon the doctrine of chances, that when all the districts are taken into computation, such difference must be equalized. The advocates of the district system, however, are the better arithmeticians. In proportion, they say, as you lessen the number of sections which elect, you multiply the chance of enabling a minority to control. On the other hand, the more numerous the sections, the fairer the representation. The probability of coming at the public will in districts is greater than that of coming at the public will in states.

In point of fact, however, the forty-eight states are not of equal size, nor do they have equal numbers of electoral votes. And this difference vitiates the whole argument. "Is it probable," asked James K. Polk, while still a member of Congress, "that there will be such a disparity, such a disproportion between the minorities of adjoining or different districts, where

---

[18] "It is merely a question whether we will divide the United States into 16 or 137 districts" (Jefferson to Monroe, January 12, 1800 [Jefferson, *Works*, IX, 90-91]).

[19] II *Register of Debates*, 1582.

[20] 102 *Congressional Record*, 5254, 5535.

all are of the same size, as would exist between the minorities of different States, differing as they do in size, some containing thirty times as great a population as others; and when, by the general system, each State would compose one district?" [21] The question was rhetorical; it had been answered a dozen years earlier by Representative William Gaston of North Carolina: "He who obtains the suffrages of more than half of the voters of the two hundred and eighteen districts into which the United States will be parceled, must in all human probability have a majority of the suffrages of the people. But how is it, sir, when each State is made to throw all its votes into one scale, however much the citizens of the State may be divided? A majority of the votes thus obtained is no evidence of the sanction of a majority of the people." [22]

A more sweeping defense of the general ticket system is offered by those who maintain that its only fault is to credit the victor in the popular election with a greater proportion of the whole number of electoral votes than he ought arithmetically to have. How often, they ask, has a man been chosen President who has not stood first in the nation-wide popular poll? Twice since the Civil War. But are two exceptions, one of which was more probably the result of fraud than arithmetic, enough to justify changing the Constitution? Indeed, could the district system promise any better results? No electoral voting system can absolutely guarantee that the popular winner will be the electoral winner. Why not then leave well enough alone and stick to a system that experience has shown to be satisfactory in its practical operation, however absurd it may be in its stipulated provisions?

This argument is all the more plausible because its fallacy

[21] II *Register of Debates*, 1646.
[22] 26 *Annals*, 839 (1814).

is deep-seated. Its error lies in the assumption that the will of the people in a national plebiscite can be ascertained by taking the will of the people in forty-eight state plebiscites. But it is a settled maxim of politics that close contests bring out the vote; one-sided contests keep it home. If the President were really elected by a national plebiscite, the incentive to vote would be of a uniform intensity throughout the country; other things being equal, we could expect the relative proportions of active voters to total population to be roughly the same in the several states. But when the contest is broken up into forty-eight parts, it will be close in some states, one-sided in others. When the popular votes in the separate states are added up, the voice of the people in the safe states will be heard much less loudly than the voice of the people in the doubtful states. A candidate favored by 51 per cent of the people in a doubtful state may overcome a candidate favored by 90 per cent of the people in a safe state of equal size solely because of the disparity in the relative turn-out of voters. We must also remember, in considering past election returns, that the arts of political management, as practiced under the general ticket system, have sometimes diverted to a third-party candidate—Weaver, for example, in 1892—votes that in a national plebiscite would have been cast for a major-party candidate. The conclusions to be drawn from the crude statistics of the popular vote in past elections are extremely limited. How can we say, for example, that Garfield and not Hancock was the choice of the people in 1880, when vast numbers of Democrats in the South were under no inducement to vote? Under a national plebiscite system might not the order of the candidates have been reversed? As things were, Garfield's proportion of the aggregate popular vote exceeded Hancock's by less than one tenth of 1 per cent. It is a great mistake to imagine that a poll taken by sections under an electoral voting system will produce the same aggregate or the same distribution of popular votes as a poll taken at large under a national plebiscite system.

Some of the arguments urged against the district system can only be characterized as indecent. That system has been denounced as unfair to the Republican party, on the ground that it is easier for that party to impress Democratic votes in the North than to win Republican votes in the South. Virginia, North Carolina, South Carolina, and Georgia, between them, have 46 votes; New York alone has 45. Under the district system it is quite conceivable that the Republicans might count 23 votes in New York and the Democrats 22; it is inconceivable, at the present time, that they could divide the votes of the four Southern states in anything like the same ratio; let it be supposed that they could win as many as 6 votes; these added to their 23 votes in New York would give them 29, but the Democrats in the five states together would count 62, a majority of 33. Under the general ticket system, however, by impressing into their own service the 22 Democratic votes of New York and surrendering to their opponents the 6 Republican votes of the South, they can count 45 votes to the Democrats' 46, a deficit of 1. The arithmetic is impeccable, but where is the justice? Why should a majority in the part prevail over the majority in the whole? To say that the Republicans are being cheated if they are required to surrender the chance of impressing large blocks of Democratic votes in the North for the chance of gaining a trivial number of Republican votes in the South is to turn morality upside down. A crooked gambler might, with as much reason, complain that the cards are stacked against him, and the game rigged, if he is compelled to deal with an honest deck.

Occasionally a post-bellum sentiment creeps into the argument. The South, which is predominantly Democratic, casts its large block of electoral votes through the agency of a very small number of voters; that is because, or partly because, it discriminates in the administration of its suffrage laws against its Negro population. The Fourteenth Amendment permits discrimination, at the price of a reduction of representation in Congress and the Electoral College; the Fifteenth Amendment forbids discrimination; but neither is in fact enforced. In this state of affairs the general ticket system, in its practical operation, takes the place of a reduction of representation, not indeed of the South but of the Democratic party as a whole. The distribution of electoral votes between the South and the rest of the country is such that the Republican party can elect its candidate not only when he is the real choice of the nation at large but sometimes when he is not; for the general ticket system enables the Republicans, upon occasion, to offset against the Democratic electoral votes of the South large blocks of Democratic votes in the North secured to them by impressment. The Democratic party, on the other hand, has no such sectional advantage, the Republican votes in the South available for impressment being so few in number. Such, however subtly it may be disguised in presentation, is the nub of the argument. Its propriety may appear in different lights to different readers. In the abstract, however, most persons may agree that the presidency, one of the most important branches of our government, ought not permanently to be founded on the principle of vengeance for past or present wrongs.

The idea that the general ticket system can be justified as compensatory of other evils appears in another shape. That system, we are told, must be preserved in the election of the President as a counterpoise to the gerrymandering system used in the election of Representatives in Congress. The present distribution of rural and urban population being assumed, the gerrymandering system operates to the advantage of the former; the general ticket system to that of the latter. If the elections to Congress are rigged in favor of the rural population, the election of the President should be rigged in favor of the urban population.

Without pausing to examine the question of whether or not control of the presidency and control of the Congress are true equivalents, and merely noticing that this line of reasoning concedes the absolute inequity of the general ticket system, we may remark that the argument can be retorted against its makers: If the election of the President is rigged in favor of the urban population, then the elections to Congress should be rigged in favor of the rural population. Such an argument, if accepted, must check all reform, and the defenders of the general ticket system for the election of the President, if they are to be true to their own logic, must associate themselves with the defenders of the gerrymandering system in the election of Representatives. This we may be certain they will not do, and the reason, I think, is clear. There have always been persons who cannot bring themselves in practice to recognize the theoretical political equality of individuals. They tend to regard the population of the country as being divided, like the characters in a Western movie, into "good guys and bad guys"—and they see nothing wrong with, indeed they applaud, a system which increases the power of their favorite group. John Randolph once defended the gerrymandering system of choosing Representatives and the general ticket system of choosing the President on the ground that this double inequity was favorable to the rural voters. It is, he said, "abhorrent to my principles that the representation in this House and the election of President should be in the ratio of a certain number of heads. . . . I am for a free, equal, republican form of Government, and I contend that nothing could be less free, nothing could be more antirepublican, than to give to the city of New York an influence on this floor, or in the Legislature of that State, which her relative numbers entitle her to." [23] What is this but a very explicit statement, with the parties reversed, of the opinions silently held by those who now denounce the gerrymandering of Congress and at the same time uphold the general ticket mode of electing the President?

Viewed in the light of the elementary principles of democracy, the adversary parties in this great dispute ought not to be looked upon as the rural population and the urban population but as one or the other of these groups against the people at large. Neither the gerrymandering system nor the general ticket system is a proper mode of election, whether for Congress or the presidency. Both systems should be abolished.

The most effective argument that has been made against the district system amendment is based on the proposition that, however skillfully it may be drawn, it cannot and will not be operated fairly; inevitably it will degenerate into a gerrymandering system. A gerrymander is an artificial arrangement of districts designed to give the political party making it more than its fair share of representation in a representative or electoral body. It is a term compounded of the name of the Governor of Massachusetts in 1812 (Elbridge Gerry) and the word "salamander," and was given to this partisan device because of the lizard-like shape of one of the senatorial districts in Massachusetts set up in that year. What, asked a Congressman in 1816, is the language of experience on this subject of districting? And he gave the answer himself: "I had, Mr. Chairman, the honor of a seat in the Legis-

[23] 30 *Annals*, 330 (1816).

lature of New York, when that State was last divided into districts for the purpose of electing members of this House. How were they laid off? With the sole view of returning as many of the supporters of Administration as possible to this House. With that view, counties were cut and slashed in every direction; districts, single, double, and treble, of every shape and of every size, were manufactured; cities were sundered, and the parts whose political character was not of the right sort were connected with counties at the distance of an hundred miles; towns were cut out of the very heart of a county, and annexed to other counties. In short, no device, however shameful, was omitted to obtain the result, and the result was obtained. For, although the great political parties were then nearly balanced in the State, yet so were the districts contrived, and so do they still exist, that not more than six or seven of the twenty-seven Representatives of that State can ever represent the wishes and opinions of the minority." [24] In the states which used the district system for the choice of Electors the story was much the same: "For the purpose of electing an Elector of President, the county of Montgomery is most unnaturally separated; a part of it, hitherto of highly Federal tone in politics, is annexed to the city of Baltimore; they are connected by a small strip of land, running the whole length of the county of Anne Arundel. Those who know the political character of Montgomery, and that of Baltimore, will be at no loss to find the inducement which led a party to force them into this unnatural alliance." [25]

Since 1949 the advocates of the proportional voting system have used this argument with much force and some justification against the plan of amendment proposed in Congress by Senator Mundt and Representative Coudert. The Mundt-

[24] 30 *Annals*, 353 (Representative Thomas P. Grosvenor).
[25] 30 *Annals*, 354 (Grosvenor).

Coudert amendment, now abandoned by its sponsors, would have required the presidential Electors to be chosen in the same manner as Senators and Representatives in Congress. But this was not a properly constructed district system amendment. The arguments in favor of it were all bottomed on the assumption that a state's Representatives in Congress would be elected on the single-member equal district system. If we read the Constitution, however, we shall find that it prescribes no uniform or fixed mode of choosing Representatives. It gives the forty-eight state legislatures almost as much power to regulate the election of Representatives as to control the appointment of Electors. They cannot, to be sure, take the election of Representatives away from the people, but they can require the elections to be made by general ticket, by multimember and unequal districts, by proportional representation, or by any combination of methods.

It is true, then, that if the Mundt-Coudert amendment were to be adopted in the form in which it was proposed, the incentives to gerrymandering might be increased. The presidency is a great prize, and much evil will be tolerated to gain it. Indeed, it is not outside the range of probability that under the Mundt-Coudert amendment, the political managers in each state might be tempted to change the mode of electing Representatives from the district system to the general ticket system. North Dakota and New Mexico now choose all their Representatives at large; other states choose some of them at large. In 1931 the legislature of Pennsylvania in a curious and backhanded manner, attempted to foist the general ticket system of electing Representatives upon the state.[26] In 1932 Virginia did in fact elect all her Representatives by that sys-

---

[26] L. F. Schmeckerbier, *Congressional Apportionment* (Washington, D. C., 1941), pp. 176-178.

tem.[27] Once started, a trend toward the general ticket system would be hard to reverse; for, as experience has shown, each state which adopted it would find its excuse in the wicked policy of its neighbor.

It would appear then that the Mundt-Coudert amendment, taken by itself, might, instead of establishing a uniform mode of electing a President by districts, begin by establishing a variety of discordant and mutable modes and end by establishing a uniform mode of electing by general ticket. Only Congress could prevent such a result. Since it has, under the Constitution, an original and concurrent power to make and alter the state regulations, it could by law require the states to use the single-member equal district system. But who can tell whether Congress, in the event, would or would not pass such a law?

The Mundt-Coudert amendment would be wholly safe only if it were coupled with another amendment requiring the states to choose their Representatives in Congress by the single-member equal district system. Such an amendment would be good in itself, and would make practicable the idea of using the congressional districts as presidential electoral districts. But it may be doubted whether an amendment with a double object could secure the necessary majorities in Congress and among the states. Experience has shown that the persons who oppose reform in the mode of choosing the President are not identical with those who oppose reform in the mode of choosing Representatives. A constitutional majority might be found in favor of each proposal separately, but together they might be defeated by a combination of two minorities.

[27] Searcy, "Congressional Redistricting in the Solid South," *Birmingham-Southern College Bulletin* (May, 1936), pp. 20-26.

This whole line of reasoning, however, goes only to prove that the Mundt-Coudert plan was not altogether soundly conceived. It has no relevance to a properly drafted amendment. Such an amendment would combat gerrymandering in two ways. In the first place it would require that the states be divided into single-member districts, such districts to consist of compact and contiguous territory and to contain, as nearly as may be, equal numbers of inhabitants. In the second place it would give to Congress the same power over the manner of holding elections for President as it now has over the manner of holding elections for Representatives. The first provision would prevent any state from establishing multi-member districts, from choosing any of its Electors at large (beyond the two corresponding to its Senators), and from laying off single-member districts of unconnected territory, queer shape, or unequal population. In short, it would set up the general standards to be followed by the state legislatures, and contingently by Congress, in marking out their electoral districts, and it would give those standards the sanction of a constitutional injunction. The second provision would enable Congress not only to correct abuses but also to give precision to the standards set up by the Constitution by regulations too detailed to find a place in the fundamental law, yet necessary if all parties are to be secured that portion of influence and power in the election of the President to which they are entitled on the basis of their numbers.

Nevertheless it has been asserted that provisions of this nature cannot be effective because they will never be enforced. "Let us examine more closely," said a very competent witness to a committee of the Senate in 1955, "this problem of gerrymandering in relation to the district plan for electing a President. It may be said that it is a problem easily remedied and that therefore the district plan should not be rejected on this ground. A brief glance at past experience, plus a dose of political realism, indicates that the contrary is true. The problem of gerrymandering is serious and virtually insurmountable. . . . The fundamental problem is not one of power to correct gerrymandering but rather of willingness to exercise that power and to back it up with effective sanctions." [28] By "past experience" the witness, Professor Dixon, was referring to the lax observance by the states of the acts passed by Congress, beginning with that of 1842, requiring the states to district themselves for the election of Representatives and containing anti-gerrymander provisions of the same type as those recommended above.

These statements are not lightly to be dismissed. Still, it is possible to answer them. As far as past experience is concerned, we must remember that the Constitution does not now prescribe any fixed method of choosing Representatives; that the act of 1842, the first exercise by Congress of its power to make regulations on this subject, was designed not so much to prevent gerrymandering as to arrest a strong trend upon the part of the states toward the general ticket system; that the states never fully admitted the power of Congress to pass a law making it obligatory on their legislatures to divide them into election districts; and that if Congress were to undertake to make the division, it would find itself involved in a task of infinite difficulty. Indeed to attempt the task would bring upon Congress the highest degree of odium, for, as a strong supporter of the district system once remarked, "it would be considered as a sort of degradation, on the part of any state, to be divided into districts, without the consent of its Legis-

[28] Evidence of Professor Robert G. Dixon, Jr. (*Nomination and Election of President and Vice President*, Hearings before a Subcommittee of the Committee on the Judiciary, U.S. Senate, 84th Cong., 1st sess., p. 197).

lature." [29] These considerations explain the fact that the anti-gerrymander laws of Congress, none of which now exist, were not found wholly efficacious. On the other hand, they did serve to prevent some of the worst abuses, and even today, in the face of congressional refusal to re-enact them, they exercise a kind of influence, monitory and minatory, upon the state legislatures that they should not too grossly depart from the rules of justice.

But past experience is not, upon this question, a proper guide to the future. We are presupposing the passage by Congress and the states of a constitutional amendment fixing the mode of electing the President by a system of equal districts. If the suffrages of two thirds of the members of both Houses of Congress and three fourths of the state legislatures can be found for such an amendment, there is some reason to hope that a majority in these bodies will not refuse to set up the machinery necessary to accomplish the amendment's object.

Such machinery would be very easy to devise. Its chief purpose should be to remove the establishment of boundaries from the immediate control of the state legislatures, even as the apportionment of Representatives among the several states has been removed from the immediate control of Congress. Just as Congress now makes the apportionment through the agency of the Bureau of the Census, a technical body, so should the state legislatures lay out the metes and bounds of their electoral districts through the agency of boundary commissions. Such commissions, constituted as nonpartisan, expert bodies, should be entrusted with the task of keeping the population movements within their respective states under review and with recommending to the several legislatures, at

[29] 30 *Annals*, 185 (Senator Dickerson). See also 33 *Annals*, 141.

each census, the alterations in constituency boundaries necessary to bring the system of districts into conformity with the injunctions of the Constitution. The recommendations of a boundary commission might, indeed, be given the force of law, unless positively rejected or amended by the state legislature itself. A boundary commission should be governed by a few general rules established by the state legislature, or Congress, or both. The normal population of a district, its electoral quota, should be defined as the number obtained by dividing the total population of the state by the number of districts to be established; varying slightly from state to state, this quota, on the basis of the 1950 census, would be approximately 342,000. Limits of toleration, say 5 or 10 per cent either way, should be set up to prevent any excessive disparities between the population of any constituency and the electoral quota for the state; if, for example, the electoral quota were 350,000 persons and the permitted variation were 10 per cent, the boundary commission could not establish a district of less than 315,000 or more than 385,000 inhabitants. The boundaries of districts should be required to be conterminous with the boundaries of existing administrative areas. If local government boundaries cannot be cut across and if the range of population permitted to a district is narrowly limited, it is difficult to see how a boundary commission, even if it were inclined to do so, could successfully practice the art and science of gerrymandering.

The procedures of a boundary commission might also be controlled by law. It should be provided with maps showing all the administrative areas in the state and the population of each. It should publish its intention to review the constituencies and name the dates upon which it will hold hearings. It should make provisional recommendations and publish them locally. It should arrange at the same time for making available for inspection by the public, at suitable places within each constituency, a copy of its proposals and a map illustrating the new area of the constituency. It should invite suggestions and objections based on its preliminary proposals and hold hearings to consider them.

A district system operated with the aid of such machinery could hardly fail to work satisfactorily. But what if, in spite of every precaution, some element of gerrymandering were to creep in? The district system would still be vastly superior to the general ticket system; for it must never be forgotten that the gerrymandering system is but an imperfect means of reaching the object set for themselves by the proponents of the general ticket system, namely the consolidation of a state's electoral votes in favor of a single candidate for President. Both are schemes of party tyranny; the idea of both is to defeat every purpose of a fair election; as between the two, that which is the least efficient is to be preferred.

It is by no means surprising that the defenders of the general ticket system have associated themselves with the advocates of the proportional voting system in equating the district to the gerrymandering system and in denouncing the latter as perfectly iniquitous. But it is somewhat remarkable to find the two groups defining its iniquity in the same way—as unfairness to minorities. In making this charge the advocates of proportional voting are speaking consistently with their principles. The defenders of the general ticket are not; for the real gravamen of their charge against the gerrymandering system is not that it is unfair to minorities but that it is not unfair enough—under it a few minority votes must necessarily escape their greedy grasp.

So much for the question of gerrymandering. Under a properly drafted constitutional amendment, supported by simple machinery, it can never present much of a problem in the election of the President. On the contrary, the existence of an equitably arranged system of districts throughout the United States, equal in number to the membership of the House of Representatives, might tend to reduce gerrymandering in the choice of Representatives by making it difficult for the states to justify the establishment of a double set of districts. The ideal to be arrived at is a system of equal districts, each choosing one Representative to Congress and each casting one electoral vote for President.

A few other objections to the district system may be briefly noticed. It has been said that the uniformity contemplated by that system is really illusory. It is all very well to fancy that the whole Union should be marked off upon the map in lots or districts of equal population, and that on the same day and in the same manner the inhabitants of each district should vote for Electors or for President. But is uniformity then obtained? "Not at all," said an early politician. "In Virginia none could vote for Electors but the landholders; while in the contiguous State of Maryland, every man above his minority would have a voice in the election. To obtain uniformity you must either force the aristocracy of Virginia to mingle their suffrages with the democracy of the State, or you must persuade the poor of Maryland to relinquish that dearest of all rights to which they have been accustomed. Where is the gentleman bold enough to hint at such an invasion of the rights of any State?" [30] Nowadays an answer might easily be found to this final question; but the point to be noticed is the irrelevance of the whole objection to the matter under discussion. The purpose of the district system is not to bring about uniformity in the suffrage laws but to produce a uniform representation of the people in the elec-

[30] 30 *Annals*, 349 (Representative Thomas P. Grosvenor of New York [1816]).

tion of the President. And in our system representation is apportioned according to population and not according to number of qualified voters or actual voters. Judged by this principle of representation, the district system would (excepting always the 96 votes to be cast by states) be completely uniform.

It has been said that the district system, however perfectly it may be arranged at any given census, must soon become unfair because of changes in the size and distribution of the national population. But surely a re-arrangement once every ten years must be thought sufficient to counteract these fluctuations. The impossibility of foreseeing them and of doing anything about them when they occur must weaken the urge to gerrymander the districts to begin with. We must recollect also that altering the districts between censuses could not increase the number of electoral votes to which a state might be entitled; and in any other point of view, it could be but of little importance.

It has been said that the district system affords inadequate representation to minor parties. The number of electoral votes obtained by such a party must depend more on the manner in which its popular votes are distributed than on their aggregate number. If its strength is concentrated in a few districts, it may win a few electoral votes; if it is dispersed over the land, it may win none. But what could be more proper if we accept the principle that the constituencies in the presidential election should be geographical rather than ideological? If the Communists cannot carry a single district, why should they receive a single district vote? On the other hand, if an equal number of voters, joined together by a community of local interests, choose to cast their electoral vote for the candidate of a minor party, why should it not be counted? Insofar as reformers are concerned, the practical alternative to district voting is proportional voting. But the proportional voting system is no more accurate than the district system when it comes to translating the popular votes for minor candidates into electoral votes. In 1948 Wallace and Thurmond each received 2.4 per cent of the popular votes cast; under the formula for proportional voting Wallace would have been credited with 1.9 per cent of the electoral votes and Thurmond with 7.1 per cent. Generally speaking, moreover, the effect of the proportional voting system must be to credit the candidates of minor parties with greater strength than they really have; for the assumption of that system is that the sentiments of the non-voters in every state are divided among the candidates in the same proportions as the sentiments of those who actually go to the polls; but that assumption is very tenuously grounded; minor parties contain a smaller ratio of indifferent members than major parties; voting as sectarians, with no other object than to show their strength in a hopeless cause, they are more apt than the major parties to bring their full numbers to the polls; the qualified voters who stay home on election day are more likely, relatively as well as absolutely, to be Republicans or Democrats than Socialists or Prohibitionists. From a theoretical point of view there is little to choose between a system that overrepresents and one that underrepresents a minor party in the electoral voting; but from a practical point of view underrepresentation is best. It is greatly to be desired that the primary election of the President should be definitive, in other words, that the choice should not devolve upon Congress; the district system is far better calculated than the proportional voting system to achieve this object.

Finally, it has been said that the district system, if extended from the election of Representatives to the election of the President, would destroy the two-party system and substitute for it a multiparty system. The argument runs somewhat as follows. At the present time a minor party lives only in the hope of winning seats in Congress. It has no hope of playing any part in the election of the President by the Electoral College, first, because it can win seats in that body only by carrying an entire state, and, second, because the general ticket system operates in such a way as invariably to give an absolute majority of the seats to one or the other of the two great parties. In this state of affairs minor parties soon wither and die; the single hope of winning seats in Congress, even when realized, is insufficient to sustain them. But under the district system the case would be different. It would be easier for a minor party to gain representation in the Electoral College; for it would need only to carry a district to win a seat. Sometimes, perhaps often, that representation could be made effective; for under the district system it might frequently happen, in closely contested elections, that neither of the great parties could win the two hundred and sixty-six seats requisite to a definitive choice. Upon such occasions the minor party Electors would hold the balance of power. They could decide in the Electoral College whether a Democrat or a Republican should be President or whether the election should be referred to Congress. In short, the possibility of playing the role of arbiter in the Electoral College would give a minor party an additional reason for existence. Moreover, the possibility of a reference to Congress would increase its desire to win seats in that body and cause it to redouble its efforts in pursuit of that object. And success in this endeavor would be a national misfortune; for any substantial increase in the number of minor party Representatives in Congress would tend to disorganize the work of Congress.

Not only, so the argument continues, would the district system encourage the minor parties to erode the great ones but also it would cause the latter to break up from within. The general ticket system gives control of the presidential contest to the Northern Democrats on the one hand and the Eastern Republicans on the other. As far as the Democrats are concerned, every Democratic victory in the twentieth century—except for Wilson's in 1916 and Truman's in 1948—has been won without the aid of Southern votes; in other words, the Northern Democrats have been able to win at least two hundred and sixty-six seats in the Electoral College from the state constituencies outside the South; in nominating their candidates for President, they have had no great political reason for taking much account of Southern views. But under the district system, the power of the Northern Democrats would be diminished. Unable to count for themselves the votes cast against them by the Republican minorities in the great states of the North, East, and West, they would have to rely on the votes cast for them in the South. As a consequence, they would have to give some consideration to Southern views. But such consideration would not be tolerated by the Northern Democrats; rather than support a candidate half-way acceptable to the South, they would form a third party. As for the Republicans, divided as they are between the urban East and rural West, the same result would follow from similar causes.

All this, it will be noticed, is speculation. But it is speculation that deserves answer; for it would be the merest folly to amend the Constitution without considering the remote as well as the immediate consequences of change. As far as the position of minor parties is concerned, it is not true that they are without hope of influencing the election of the President at the present time. Granted that the general ticket system tends to prevent them from winning enough seats in the Electoral College to determine the election or throw it into Congress, the same system permits them to play the role of arbiter much more effectively at an earlier stage. If they can seldom hope to decide the election in December at the meetings of the Electoral College, they can often hope to decide it in November in New York or in one of the other great doubtful states. In those states, when the great parties are evenly matched, a minor party may have it in its power to consolidate the electoral votes of the entire state and to give them to whichever of the two major parties it prefers. To exchange the general ticket for the district system would, insofar as a minor party is concerned, be to exchange a greater for a lesser expectation. If the former cannot now keep the party alive, how will the latter do it?

This branch of the argument is, moreover, grounded on a supposition as to the details of a district system amendment that will probably not be realized. In the debates on the Lodge-Gossett resolution of 1950 and the Daniel-Mundt resolution of 1956, it became clear that any plan designed to bring the electoral results more closely in correspondence with the real divisions of the people would be accompanied by a proviso making something less than an absolute majority sufficient for a definitive election. A district system amendment will probably be so drawn as to prevent the exercise by the House of Representatives of its eventual power if less than a majority but not less than a designated percentage, say 40 per cent, of the electoral votes are cast for the same person. With such a proviso, the district system, if established, would be no more likely to result in an inconclusive primary election than the general ticket system is now. Recognizing this fact, the defenders of the general ticket system answer it as follows: If the number of votes requisite to a definitive election is reduced from 266 to 213, the need for political compromise within each of the great parties will be reduced; the dominant groups in each party will pay less attention to the views of minorities; and the latter will tend to fly off. To this allegation two answers may be returned. In the first place, we must always remember that a political party, under the present system, in seeking 266 votes does not base its calculations solely upon the numbers of its own adherents. If it expects to carry New York in the ratio of 23 to 22, it counts for itself the 22 minority votes which, under the district system, might be cast against it; much less intra-party accommodation may be needed to collect 266 votes under the general ticket system than to collect 213 votes under the district system. In the second place, it is a mistake to assume that a political party will be satisfied to seek only 213 votes. Forty per cent of the whole number of electoral votes may be sufficient to determine the election, but it does not follow that 213 votes will be sufficient for the election of a particular candidate; even a candidate who polls 265 votes will be beaten by one who polls 266. An absolute majority must remain the goal of every party with a chance of victory.

The idea that the great parties will split in two if the district system is established seems equally ill-founded. The line of reasoning by which it is supported seems far better calculated to prove that they are about to break up now as a consequence of the general ticket system. Let us look at the Democratic party. Under the district system its non-Southern sections would be compelled, in the choice of a candidate, to accommodate—but not surrender—their views to those of the South; under the general ticket system they are under no such compulsion. The district system must produce a national candidate; the general ticket system, a non-Southern one. If we feel that the non-Southern Democrats will split the party rather than support a national candidate, how can we be sure that the Southern Democrats will support a non-Southern candidate rather than split the party?

Such are the arguments that have been brought to bear against the passage of a district system amendment. That they are not consistent with each other is natural. Considered separately, none of them is well-founded. It remains only to suggest the wording of a satisfactory resolution. Something like the following might do:

> For the purpose of choosing a President and Vice President of the United States, each State shall be divided by the Legislature thereof into as many districts as will equal the number of Representatives to which such State may be entitled in Congress, and each district shall be composed of contiguous and compact territory and contain, as nearly as may be, the number of persons which entitles the State to a Representative in Congress according to the apportionment; which districts, when laid off, shall not be altered until after another census shall have been taken.
>
> The inhabitants of each of the said districts, who shall have the qualifications requisite for electors of the most numerous branch of the State Legislature, shall choose one Elector of President and Vice President. The inhabitants of each State, having the same qualifications, shall choose two Electors of President and Vice President.
>
> The places and manner of holding elections for Electors of President and Vice President shall be prescribed in each State by the Legislature thereof; but the Congress may at any time by law make or alter such regulations.

These provisions, joined to the sections of the existing Constitution which prescribe the manner of voting in the Electoral College, would be sufficient to establish a uniform method of voting by districts for the President. Whether it would be advisable to change that provision of the Constitution which makes an absolute majority of the whole number of electoral votes necessary to a definitive choice, is a question that we shall take up in a later chapter. We shall look next at the idea of abolishing the Electors altogether and permitting the people of each constituency to cast their electoral votes for President directly instead of through an agency.

8. *The Intermediate Electors*

Any electoral voting system can be worked with or without the agency of intermediate Electors. Were the general ticket system to be established by constitutional amendment, it would be easy enough to provide that the qualified voters in each state should give their suffrages directly to the candidate of their choice, and that the person receiving the greatest number of such suffrages in any given state should be credited with the whole number of that state's electoral votes. Likewise, under the district system, the distribution of a state's electoral votes among the several candidates could be committed to a direct vote of the people; it would only be necessary to provide that the person receiving the greatest number of popular votes for President in each district should be holden to have received one electoral vote, and that the person receiving the greatest number of popular votes in each state should be holden to have received two electoral votes. Conversely, the proportional voting system could be operated without abolishing the Electoral College; it would be sufficient to elect each state's delegation in that body by the methods of proportional representation.

The idea of retaining the electoral voting system, but discontinuing the use of intermediate Electors, is an old one.

First advanced in the shape of a constitutional amendment by Senator Benton of Missouri in 1823,[1] it had long been hinted at. In 1801 Jefferson wrote to Gallatin of an "amendment which I know will be proposed, to wit, to have no electors, but let the people vote directly, and the ticket which has a plurality of the votes of any state to be considered as receiving the whole vote of the state."[2] And in 1803 Representative James Holland declared that he would "have preferred an immediate suffrage to this indirect mode of election by electors."[3]

The argument which is usually brought forward to support the proposal is very plausible, if not altogether sound. I give it in the words of the Report of a Select Committee of the Senate made January 19, 1826: "It was the intention of the Constitution that these electors should be an independent body of men, chosen by the People from among themselves, on account of their superior discernment, virtue, and information; and that this select body should be left to make the election according to their own will, without the slightest

[1] H. V. Ames, *Proposed Amendments to the Constitution of the United States*, p. 89. Benton himself asserted the novelty of his proposal (41 *Annals*, 168). His was a district system amendment.

[2] Jefferson to Gallatin, September 18, 1801 (Jefferson, *Works*, IX, 305). Such an amendment would have fixed the general ticket system on the states. The Norris amendment of 1934, as finally voted on by the Senate, was of the same type. So was the Kennedy amendment of 1957.

[3] 13 *Annals*, 735. Holland may have wanted to abolish the electoral votes as well as the Electors, but as he came from North Carolina, this is unlikely. He probably had in mind, insofar as his own state was concerned, a direct vote of the people in districts, as later proposed by Senator Benton. Possibly he would have accepted the scheme of Representative Charles Kellogg of New York, who in 1826 proposed to abolish the Electors and to leave to the states the task of collecting their electoral votes "in such a manner as their Legislatures shall direct" (II *Register of Debates*, 1858).

control from the body of the People. That this intention has failed of its object in every election, is a fact of such universal notoriety, that no one can dispute it. . . . Electors, therefore, have not answered the design of their institution. They are not the independent body and superior characters which they were intended to be. They are not left to the exercise of their own judgment; on the contrary they give their vote, or bind themselves to give it, according to the will of their constituents. They have degenerated into mere agents, in a case which requires no agency, and where the agent must be useless, if he is faithful, and dangerous, if he is not. Instead of being chosen for their noble qualities set forth in the *Federalist*, candidates for electors are now most usually selected for their devotion to a party, their popular manners, and a supposed talent at electioneering, which the framers of the Constitution would have been ashamed to possess." [4]

There are some things about this argument which call for comment. While it is doubtless true that the character of the Electors has sunk from the standard of perfection visualized by the framers of the Constitution, it is very doubtful that these Electors were ever intended to act a part wholly independent of the people. The electoral system was the invention, not of that part of the Federal Convention which distrusted the people, but of that part which trusted them. In our first chapter we have collected the evidences that the mode adopted was considered by the Founding Fathers an equivalent to an election by the people. Their statements would be meaningless had they intended the Electoral College to operate independently of the people. A pseudonymous

---

[4] II *Register of Debates*, Appendix, p. 121. That Benton was the author of this report can be proved by comparing this passage with his speech of January 30, 1824 (41 *Annals*, 178).

writer in the *Aurora,* explaining the electoral system in 1796, expounded the relationship of the people to the Electors in terms which the framers must have approved: "The President must not be merely the creature of a spirit of accommodation or intrigue among the electors. The electors should be the faithful agents of the people in this important business; act in their behalf as the people would act were the President and Vice President elected immediately by them; and to this end the people must make up individually their own minds upon the merits of the two candidates. The electors must become acquainted with the sentiments of their constituents, and the people come to a knowledge of the opinions of the electoral candidates, that in exercising the important right of voting, they do not place their confidence in one who shall, in the only act required of him give his vote in opposition to their views and interests. Let the people then choose their electors with a view to the ultimate choice." [5]

All this is not to say that the Electors were intended to be mere agents without discretion, pledged automata whose later votes would be known at the moment of their appointment. The provisions of the Constitution requiring the Electors to vote *by ballot* [6] and to *seal* up and transmit their votes to the President of the Senate, together with the provision requiring the House of Representatives, in certain contingencies, *immediately* to choose the President, prove, as Charles Pinckney once remarked, that the votes were meant to be "secret and

[5] Quoted from Charles A. O'Neil, *The American Electoral System* (New York, 1887), pp. 55-56. Mr. O'Neil regarded this appeal as foreshadowing the complete prostration of the plan of the Fathers, "in the transformation of the ideal elector into a mere instrument to record the will of those who chose him"—a remark that the Fathers would have found surprising.

[6] "We all know that to vote by ballot is to vote secretly" (Charles Pinckney, 10 *Annals,* 139).

unknown until opened in the presence of both Houses." [7]
But in considering this matter we must always remember the
act required of the Electors: They were to name, not one, but
two men for President, and of these at least one must not be an
inhabitant of the same state with themselves. As we have seen,
many members of the Federal Convention expected the Electors to cast the first of their votes for a state favorite and the
second for a continental character. As to the state favorite,
they could scarcely be in doubt as to the will of their constituents, but as to the continental character, they were expected to supply the ignorance of their constituents by their
own information and vote for the man who might be called the
people's presumptive favorite. Furthermore, the Electors were
not allowed to discriminate in their votes between the person intended by them to be President and the person intended
to be Vice President; both votes were expected to be counted
equally in the making of a President, and this was to introduce
an element of lottery into the election. It might easily happen
that when the votes were opened in Congress, two candidates
might be tied with a majority or no candidate might have a
majority. By requiring the votes of the Electors to be concealed "in midnight silence and secrecy," it was hoped to
prevent the agencies of corruption, especially foreign powers,
from discovering the names of the two, or five, individuals
from amongst whom the House of Representatives might be
compelled to choose. To prevent corruption when the facts
were known was the object of requiring the House to proceed immediately to the contingent election.

That the Electors exercised a certain amount of discretion
in fact, prior to the passage of the Twelfth Amendment, appears certain. In 1792 the North Carolina Electors debated

[7] 10 *Annals*, 138.

the respective merits of George Clinton and John Adams and finally decided to support the former.[8] In the same year the Virginia Electors "opened their doors and held debates and made philippics before the *Marseillois*," by which means 6 votes were said to have been converted from Adams to Clinton.[9] In 1796 and 1800 the Electors in several states discussed the number of votes that they would throw away from the man intended by them for Vice President, but not the number of votes that they would give to their bona fide candidate for President.[10] These instances, however, merely prove the failure of the double voting system. The debates of 1792 had to do only with the selection of a Vice President, a topic which the Electors were not constitutionally authorized to discuss. Those of 1796 and 1800 had to do with the problem of bringing in the two candidates of the same party in a particular order, an objective likewise inconsistent with the design of the original Constitution.

With the abolition of the double voting system in 1804, the Electors lost, in fact, all discretion and became mere mouthpieces of their constituencies. But this change in their character was slight, and ought to be accounted a fulfillment rather than a failure of the intention of the Constitution; for, let us repeat, the Electors were never meant to choose the President but only to pronounce the votes of the people.

No argument for abolishing the Electors can be based on their personal characters. It may very well be true that the

[8] O'Neil, *American Electoral System*, p. 48.

[9] *Letters of John Adams Addressed to His Wife* (Boston, 1841), p. 118.

[10] An account of the debates in the Connecticut Electoral College is given in a letter from Oliver Wolcott to his son, December 12, 1796 (George Gibbs, *Memoirs of the Administrations of Washington and Adams* [New York, 1846], I, 408-410).

Electors of today are less distinguished and less able persons than they were in the beginning. The roster of Electors in our first elections reads like a "Who's Who in the State Governments." [11] As late as 1855 it was noticed that in Alabama and Mississippi the ablest men of the state were Electors and went among the people to instruct, excite, and arouse them upon the issues between the parties.[12] Today not one man in ten thousand knows who the Electors are. But, in any point of view except electioneering, the character of an Elector is unimportant. The fact has long been recognized. In 1819 Senator James Barbour of Virginia defined an Elector as a man "who has but one insulated duty to perform, that of voting for the character his constituents prefer, as President, and of whom a pledge is always required, and indeed given, before he is supported by the people." And he concluded that "in effect, it is of little consequence who is selected, as he serves only as an organ, to convey the wishes of his constituents to the Electoral college. He furnishes the only requisite, by the pledge he previously gives of supporting the man of their choice." [13]

To knock out or weaken the historical argument for abolishing the Electors is not, of course, to touch the substantive argument. It might still be true that the Electors are agents in a case that requires no agency, and that they are useless if they are faithful and dangerous if they are not. On the other hand, it might appear that the dangers are exaggerated and the utility minimized. Granted that an Elector might be faithless to his trust, it does not follow that no trust should be committed to him. Granted that he is the mere mouthpiece of

[11] The names of the Electors, with some inaccuracies, will be found in the various editions of Lanman's *Dictionary of Congress*.

[12] *South Carolina Legislative Times*, December 7, 1855, p. 84.

[13] 33 *Annals*, 153 (1819).

his constituents, it may still be thought that a mouthpiece is a very useful instrument.

Since the beginning of the government there are but two instances in which it can be clearly shown that an Elector has voted for someone other than the person to whom he was pledged. And neither of these instances presented the slightest danger to our institutions. In 1820 William Plumer, a former Senator from New Hampshire, voted for John Quincy Adams instead of Monroe, and in 1956 a man named Turner voted for Circuit Judge Jones instead of Stevenson. But these votes were given in elections that were already determined and exhibit a mere eccentricity on the part of those who gave them. Plumer was too honorable a man to have violated his pledge, if violation would have changed the result of the contest.[14] Turner, if we may judge by his statement of justification,[15] lacked some of the qualities of a man who would dare to set his will against the will of the nation.

The other instances in which a betrayal of trust has been alleged are not so clear. In 1796 a Pennsylvania Elector, pledged under the double voting system to Adams and Pinckney, voted instead for Pinckney and Jefferson; he elicited the famous remark of a Federalist voter: "Do I choose Samuel Miles to determine for me whether John Adams or Thomas

[14] "As presidential elector in 1820, Plumer cast the single vote against James Monroe, not, as has so often been stated, to protect Washington's fame as the only President to receive the unanimous electoral vote, but to draw attention to his friend John Quincy Adams, for whom he voted, and as a protest against what he regarded as the wasteful extravagance of the Monroe Administration" (Everett S. Brown, *William Plumer's Memorandum of Proceedings in the United States Senate* [New York, 1923], p. vii).

[15] "I have fulfilled my obligations to the people of Alabama. I'm talking about the white people" (*New York Times*, December 18, 1956).

Jefferson is the fittest man for President of these United States? No, I choose him to act, not to think." [16] But Miles might have made a satisfactory reply. The Federalists, expecting to carry the state, had insisted that the vote be taken by general ticket; they had even declared the district system unconstitutional, on the ground that every voter was empowered by that instrument to vote for every Elector to which the state was entitled; but Pennsylvania had voted Republican, and Miles had secured his seat only by a political accident—the holding back, it was said, of the Greene County returns. Miles might, with some justice, have claimed that, in these circumstances, the will of his constituents, the people of Pennsylvania at large, pointed to Jefferson, and that by his vote he truly conveyed it. The whole incident is very obscure; but it is certain that the Eastern Federalists feared they would lose the votes of both their Pennsylvania Electors. [17]

The historian McMaster has charged the North Carolina Electors of 1824 with a breach of trust because they did not divide their votes between Adams and Jackson but cast them all for Jackson. These Electors, he tells us, were chosen on an anti-Crawford general ticket; each voter was instructed to write the name of Adams or Jackson across the printed names of the Electors, and the Electors were to give their votes in proportion to the relative strength of the two candidates, as thus ascertained; about a third of the anti-Crawford voters favored Adams, and consequently he should have received 5 electoral votes from North Carolina.[18] It would appear, however, that McMaster did not correctly understand the nature of the fusion agreement: The Electors were to vote

---

[16] O'Neil, *American Electoral System*, p. 65.

[17] Gibbs, *Administrations*, I, 400, 402.

[18] J. B. McMaster, *A History of the United States* (New York, 1904), V, 74-75

as a bloc for the more popular candidate; and before election all but three had declared for Jackson.[19]

McMaster and others have also accused three New York Electors, pledged to Clay, with a similar breach of trust in the same election. Had these three Electors voted for Clay (instead of dividing their votes between Jackson, Adams, and Crawford) Clay and Crawford would have been tied for third place; both would have come before the House of Representatives at the contingent election; and Clay might have been chosen President. The facts, however, were not quite as stated. The New York state legislature had appointed as Electors twenty-five Adams men, four Crawford men, and seven Clay men; these Clay men had run on a Crawford-Clay fusion slate in the Senate and an Adams-Clay fusion slate in the House, and were, of course, chosen Electors on the first ballot when the two Houses met to compose their differences. But one of the Clay Electors, Timothy H. Porter of Cattaraugus, did not vote as an Elector, having been chosen a Representative in Congress; his place was supplied by William Mann of Schoharie, the election being made by the Electors themselves; Mann, it may be presumed, was a supporter of Adams, and gave him his twenty-sixth vote. It is not true, therefore, that the Clay Electors in New York could have brought his name before the House; nor do his contemporary biographers make the claim.[20] Clay's chances in the Electoral College depended on the outcome of the vote for Electors in the Louisiana legislature; that outcome was known before the meeting of the New York Electors—Clay had been defeated by a parliamentary trick played by the supporters of

[19] A. R. Newsome, *The Presidential Election of 1824 in North Carolina* (Chapel Hill, 1939), Chap. VIII.

[20] Epes Sargent, *Henry Clay* (New York, 1848), p. 36n. Calvin Colton, *Henry Clay* (New York, 1846), p. 292.

Adams and Jackson. The Clay Electors, now only six in number, considered themselves as released from their pledge and voted as whim or conscience dictated—four for Clay, one for Crawford, and one for Jackson.

When fusion tickets are presented to the people, it is not always very clear for whom the Electors of the minority faction are expected to vote. In 1948 the successful Democratic ticket in Tennessee was composed of ten men pledged to Truman and two who had previously announced their intention of voting for Thurmond and who were, in fact, also running on a straight Thurmond ticket. If the votes of these Thurmond Electors could have influenced the outcome of the election, would anyone have been surprised if they had cast them in the best interests of the States' Rights party? In the actual event, since their votes were ineffective, one voted for Truman and the other for Thurmond.

One other case remains to be considered. During the debates on the Lodge-Gossett resolution in 1951, it was frequently asserted that Jefferson had been cheated out of the presidency in 1796 by the infidelity of three Republican Electors, one in North Carolina, one in Virginia, and one in Massachusetts. This allegation has no basis in fact and appears to be based on a faulty understanding of the electoral system and of the political principles of the condemned Electors. In Virginia one electoral vote was, indeed, cast for Adams; it was the vote of Levin Powell of Upperville; but Powell was a Federalist chosen under the Virginia district system from a Federalist district.[21] In North Carolina the election was also by districts, and the Federalist vote was a bona

---

[21] V *Register of Debates*, 123. The Federalists had relied on two votes in Virginia and hoped for two others (Gibbs, *Administrations*, II, 402).

fide one.[22] The Massachusetts Elector was Elbridge Gerry, later Vice President of the United States under Madison. But Gerry was chosen to vote for Adams and did so. In a letter to Jefferson he made his position clear: "Permit me, with great sincerity to congratulate you on your appointment to the office of Vice President of the United States. It was in my mind a very desirable object, and a wish which I ardently expressed at the meeting of the Electors; but, as we were unanimously of opinion that Mr. Adams' pretensions to the chair were best, it was impossible to give you any votes without annulling an equal number for him." [23]

It would appear, then, that there is little to be feared from an abuse of trust on the part of the Electors. But are they useful? Madison, consulted on this point in 1825, had this to say: "One advantage of Electors is, that although generally the mere mouths of their Constituents, they may be intentionally left sometimes to their own judgment, guided by further information that may be acquired by them: and finally, what is of material importance, they will be able,

[22] Gibbs, *Administrations*, I, 402. The Federalist elector was a "man of no consideration." It was feared that the publication of Adet's note might change the opinion of his ignorant and fickle constituents and that he might follow it. But he voted for Adams.

[23] Elbridge Gerry to Thomas Jefferson, March 27, 1797 (James Austin, *Life of Elbridge Gerry* [Boston, 1828], II, 134-135). Gerry was considered a Federalist as late as 1800 (Theophilus Parsons to John Jay, May 5, 1800 [*The Correspondence and Public Papers of John Jay*, H. P. Johnston, ed. (New York, 1890-1893), IV, 168]). A Maryland Elector named Plater did in fact vote for both Adams and Jefferson in 1796. He was probably a Federalist, since that party was counting on, and actually received, 7 electoral votes from that state (Gibbs, *Administrations*, I, 201). O'Neil, however, says he was a Republican (*American Electoral System*, p. 66). Paullin's *Atlas of the Historical Geography of the United States* maps his district as Federalist.

when ascertaining, which may not be till a late hour, that the first choice of their constituents is utterly hopeless, to substitute in the electoral vote the name known to be their second choice." [24]

There have been cases where exactly this course has been followed. In 1824, as we have seen, the Electors of North Carolina were pledged both to Jackson and Adams with the understanding that they would vote for the one who had the best chance of success. And as recently as 1912 the Roosevelt ticket of Electors in South Dakota declared before election that if Theodore Roosevelt could not be elected and it should become a contest between Taft and Wilson, they would vote for Taft. [25]

A second advantage of Electors is that they act as a connecting link between the presidency and vice presidency. Since they are pledged to support the candidates of their parties for both offices, it can seldom happen that the popular election will result in the choice of a President of one party and a Vice President of another. It is conceivable, however, that in a close election without Electors a popular vice-presidential candidate of a minority party might succeed where his principal failed. The Twelfth Amendment to the Constitution, it will be remembered, was adopted precisely to prevent such a result.

Against these advantages there are, to be sure, disadvantages. Perhaps the most serious is this. The use of intermediate Electors, especially under the general ticket system, limits the choice of voters in each state to those candidates who

[24] Madison to Robert Taylor, January 30, 1826 (Madison, *Writings*, IX, 150n.).

[25] C. O. Paullin, *Atlas of the Historical Geography of the United States*, p. 103.

have electoral tickets, and, more particularly, to those candidates whose electoral tickets appear on the printed ballots and voting machines. In 1856, for example, it proved impossible for the voters in most of the Southern states to cast a single vote for Frémont and Dayton. In 1912 a Californian could vote for Taft and his unnamed colleague [26] only by writing in the names of thirteen Electors. In 1948 the Alabama voters were precluded from voting for Truman and Barkley.

It would appear then that the desirability of abolishing the intermediate Electors is not quite so self-evident as it seemed at first glance. What should be done depends mainly on what changes are made in other parts of the electoral system. Principally, as we shall see in the next chapter, it depends on whether or not some proper mode is introduced of taking the sense of the nation in cases where the electoral voting has been inconclusive. With such a mode most of the advantages of Electors would disappear. Without it, the case might be different.

One reform might, however, be made if the Constitution is amended and the Electors retained. The words *by ballot* might be struck out of that part of the Twelfth Amendment which prescribes the mode of voting in the Electoral College. The notion that the votes of the Electors can be kept secret until they are opened in Congress is impossible of fulfillment. As early as 1803, a Congressman remarked that a recurrence to all the elections for President and Vice President since the commencement of the government would "fully demonstrate that the person intended by the Electors to fill each office was well understood and known to all the Electors, and to all

[26] The Republican candidate for Vice President died before election day. It was not until after the election that the Republican National Committee determined that the Republican Electors should vote for Nicholas Murray Butler.

other persons who wish to know the secret has not been kept." [27] In 1800 a New York Elector, Anthony Lispenard, is said to have stood on his right, or rather his duty, to cast a secret vote. It was suspected, however, that he intended to drop Jefferson and cast his double vote for Burr and some indifferent character—a maneuver that would have made Burr President. De Witt Clinton, "a discerning citizen," therefore attended the meeting of the Electors, and, though not one of them, so far overawed them as to persuade them to show each other their ballots anterior to their being deposited in the ballot box. Lispenard hesitated but, finding his colleagues unanimous and pertinacious in their determination, at length exhibited his ballot after marking it for Jefferson and Burr.[28] At the present time, in at least seventeen states, the Electors do not in fact vote by ballot, in the constitutional meaning of the term, but announce orally or by signature the person for whom they vote.[29] A constitutional provision that has not, and never will, answer its design, might well be dropped.

[27] 13 *Annals*, 736 (James Holland).

[28] James Cheetham to Thomas Jefferson, December 10, 1801 (*Proceedings of the Massachusetts Historical Society*, 3d Series, I, 47).

[29] Robert G. Dixon, "Electoral College Procedure," *Western Political Quarterly* (June, 1950), pp. 220-221.

9. The Contingent Election

The Twelfth Amendment to the Constitution provides that the person having the greatest number of electoral votes for President shall be the President if such number be a majority of the whole number of Electors appointed; but if no person have such majority, then the House of Representatives, voting by states and not by heads, shall immediately, by ballot, choose the President "from the persons having the highest numbers not exceeding three on the list of those voted for as President." A quorum for the purpose consists of a member or members from two thirds of the states, and a majority of all the states is necessary to a choice. This amendment differs from the original Constitution, insofar as the contingent election of the President is concerned, only in respect of the number of persons to whom the choice is confined; prior to the election of 1804, in cases of no majority, the House might have chosen from the five persons highest on the list. The possibility of two or three persons being tied with a majority disappeared with the abolition of the double vote for President.

The impropriety of the mode of voting by states has long been noticed. George Mason and others made it a ground of objection to ratifying the Constitution. Madison, though he gave that mode his approbation in the Virginia Convention of 1788, at a later date spoke against it in no uncertain terms: "The present rule of voting for President by the House of Representatives is so great a departure from the Republican principle of numerical equality, and even from the federal rule which qualifies the numerical by a State equality, and is so pregnant also with a mischievous tendency in practice, that an amendment of the Constitution on this point is justly called for by all its considerate and best friends."[1] Others have harped on the injustice of a system which makes a single member from one state equal to forty-three members from another.

The rule of voting in the House has also been denounced on purely theoretical grounds. "There cannot," said McDuffie of South Carolina in 1826, "be a greater political solecism than that which is involved in the idea of commencing the election of the President upon one principle, and ending it according to another. If the popular principle is the true principle of this election, as indicated by the Constitution itself, nothing can be more absurd than to abandon it entirely as soon as the People, at the first effort, fail to give a majority of votes for one candidate. It looks like punishing the People, by forfeiture, for not being more unanimous."[2]

Unfair and absurd, these are the epithets that come naturally to the tongue when we contemplate the rule of equal voting. But it is also impracticable. Let us look for a moment at the difficulty of coming to a decision under it. We may take the case where three persons have been nominated to the House, none of whom is supported by the representations of twenty-five states. A state vote, under the rules of the House

[1] Madison to George Hay, August 23, 1823 (Madison, *Writings*, IX, 151).
[2] II *Register of Debates*, 1945.

adopted in 1801 and 1825, is ascertained by polling the individual members of the state delegations. To fix our ideas, let it be supposed that eighteen states vote Democratic, seventeen Republican, and thirteen Dixiecrat. How are 25 votes to be obtained for any one candidate? Plainly, some states must change their votes. But which states? It must be remembered that since the adoption in 1933 of an amendment changing the beginning of the President's term from March 4 to January 20, the eventual choice is to be made by the newly elected House; it is certain that the failure of the Electoral College to choose will have been foreseen, and that the members of the House of Representatives will have been elected with an eye, not so much to their individual merits, as to their contingent faculty as Electors of the President. Assurances will have been asked and given. In these circumstances every Representative will feel with peculiar force the conflict between the injunction of the Constitution immediately to choose a President and the presumptive instructions of his constituents to vote for a particular candidate.

Nor is this the only difficulty. The rules that govern the contingent election are such that even if the choice were confined to two persons, it would be hard to make. The single vote of a state is indivisible. It cannot be distributed fractionally between the several candidates favored by the individual members of a state delegation; nor can it be ascertained by the votes of a simple plurality of the delegation. Unless one candidate has an absolute majority of the significant [3] individual votes of a delegation, the state ballot is

---

[3] Significant votes are to be distinguished from blank votes and uncast votes. The majority required in ascertaining the vote of a state is not that of the entire authorized membership of its delegation but that of the members present and voting for a particular person. The election of 1801 was determined, not by changed votes, but

marked *divided* and is counted for no one. In 1801 Jefferson needed 9 state votes in order to defeat Burr. For 35 ballotings he received 8 votes and Burr 6; the two remaining votes—those of Vermont and Maryland—were counted for neither, the individual votes of the Representatives from each of these states having been equally divided between the two candidates. In 1825 Adams needed 13 state votes to defeat Jackson and Crawford. Everything depended on the vote of New York, the representation of which consisted of thirty-four members. In ascertaining the vote of the state, eighteen members voted for Adams, fourteen for Crawford, and two for Jackson; the name of Adams was accordingly written on the New York ballot; but if Stephen Van Rensselaer, the patroon, had voted, as he was expected to vote, for Crawford instead of Adams, the New York ballot would have been marked *divided*, and the first balloting of the House would have been inconclusive.

In derogation of these observations it is not sufficient to say that the experience of two trials demonstrates that, in one way or another, the House of Representatives will always contrive to do its constitutional duty and elect a President. The cases of 1801 and 1825 were both peculiar, and the former cannot be repeated. In 1801 Burr was not a bona fide candidate for the presidency; he was the Republican candidate for Vice President, placed by a political accident in competition with his chief, and taken up as a presidential candidate by the Federalists in Congress, against the advice of the wisest heads in that party. In 1825 four candidates had received votes in the Electoral College, and all of them had

because on the thirty-sixth trial some of Burr's supporters withdrew and others cast blank ballots, a procedure which produced a majority for Jefferson in the representations of Vermont and Maryland, which had previously been divided.

supporters in the House of Representatives; but one of them, Clay, had been eliminated by the "rule of three." His supporters, very numerous in the House, were free agents, available to make up a majority for some other candidate on the first balloting. Another candidate, Crawford, had been for nearly two years a paralytic; his condition had been misrepresented to the public, but in Congress it was known that there was no probability of his restoration to such a measure of health as would enable him to exercise the presidential office. His election in these circumstances would have been an imposition on the public; it would have served only to bring in the Vice President, Calhoun, as acting President. The supporters of Crawford in the House must, therefore, also be regarded as free agents. They gave their votes to their nominal candidate on the first and only balloting, but it was generally understood that had further ballotings been needed, some of them would have switched to Adams. In reality, then, the election of 1825 resolved itself into a contest between only two candidates—Adams and Jackson. It was all the easier to resolve because so many Representatives were in a position to cast their individual ballots without fear of reprisal from their constituents. Indeed, in 1825, the state of parties was such that if Clay rather than Crawford had been the third candidate, the supporters of Adams or Jackson might in the end have switched their votes to him. They could have said, in justification of such a step, that they had not been elected with reference to the presidential question, that the necessity of making an *immediate* choice of itself excluded the idea of any interference of their constituents by instruction, that the right of choosing implies the right of selection, and that if they were not to act wholly from the cool dictates of their judgment, they were to vote their constituents' second choices if their first could not prevail.[4] In future elections the situation of a Representative called upon to choose a President will not be so easy. More or less pledged in advance to vote for a particular candidate, he will find it hard to explain why he voted for someone else.

All this is not to suggest that the House will refuse to elect a President when the choice devolves upon it. The language of the Constitution is imperative: The power to choose is also the duty to choose. We have no right to assume that the individual members will go on to the end, voting as they began, and so defeat the election. Were they to do so, the whole business of the House would be arrested—and arrested for four years; for there is nothing in the Constitution that sets a terminal date to the ballotings. The Twentieth Amendment, indeed, clearly contemplates that these may continue beyond the day (January 20) set for the beginning of the President's term. But who can suppose that the country would tolerate a situation in which no revenue bills could be originated, no appropriation or legislative bills passed, no impeachment proceedings initiated—a situation, in short, where the Executive Department (under an acting President) and the Senate were the only operating branches of the government? Public opinion would soon force the Representatives to settle upon one of the candidates before them; it would not admit the excuse that they were bound indefinitely by their consciences or the assurances that they might in November have given to their constituents.

But it *is* conceivable that the House might refuse to choose for fourteen days. The Twentieth Amendment provides that

[4] The question of how far a Representative was to be guided by his conscience and how far by the presumed will of his constituents was debated at some length in 1825 (I *Register of Debates*, 420-434, 445-461, 491-514).

if a President shall not have been chosen by January 20, the Vice President-elect shall act as President until a President shall have qualified. And it is almost certain that there will be a Vice President-elect; for the choice of this officer, if it has not already been made by the Electoral College, is committed by the Twelfth Amendment to the Senate voting by heads, and is confined to the persons having the *two* highest numbers on the list. No doubt it would be a dereliction of duty if the Representatives were to vote with the intention of bringing the Vice President in. "There is no man," said McDuffie in 1825, "whom I would prefer to the individual [Calhoun] designated by the people for the office of Vice President. But, sir, if, under the influence of this feeling, I were to give my vote in this House, for the indirect purpose of defeating the election, and throwing upon the Vice-President elect powers which the people never intended to confer; though my vote and my motive should be concealed from every human eye, I should never be able to make peace with my own conscience." [5] But to some these notions of morality may appear quixotic. The Vice President-elect will be of the same party as one of the presidential candidates. May not the supporters of that candidate in the House be willing to stop the wheels of government for fourteen days if, by so doing, they can, on the fifteenth day, bring to bear upon the election the full force of the executive patronage and influence?

Considerations such as these were perhaps in Jefferson's mind when in 1823 he told his friend George Hay that he had "ever considered the constitutional mode of election ultimately by the legislature voting by States as the most dan-

[5] I *Register of Debates,* 454.

gerous blot in our Constitution, and one which some unlucky
chance will some day hit, and give us a pope and anti-pope." [6]
Be that as it may, it is certain that few statesmen have defended a principle that levels the power of the states, penalizes
the people for expressing too great a diversity of opinion, and
can only with the greatest difficulty be reduced to practice. [7]
Many statesmen, on the other hand, have advocated reform.

The simplest remedy would certainly be that advocated by
Senator Lodge of Massachusetts in 1948 and, before him, by
many others: Let the person having the greatest number of
electoral votes for President be the President. High authority
can be quoted for the idea of making a plurality sufficient
to elect. James Wilson, perhaps the leading member of the
Federal Convention, when the subject was under debate, once
declared that "the concurrence of a majority of people is
not a necessary principle of election, nor required as such in
any of our States." Mason and Williamson "preferred making
the highest though not having a majority of the votes, President, to a reference of the matter to the Senate." Madison
and Williamson moved to strike out the word "majority" and
insert "one third" so that "the eventual power might not be
exercised if less than a majority but not less than one third
of the Electors should vote for the same person."

High authority and strong arguments, however, can likewise be brought forward to sustain a different view. The
members of the Federal Convention as a body decided that
a majority vote would be necessary for the choice of a

[6] Jefferson to George Hay, August 17, 1823 (Jefferson, *Works*, XII,
303). Backgammon players will understand the meaning of "hitting
a blot."

[7] Senator Benton of Missouri is an exception. In 1824 he defended
the equal vote; but in 1826 a committee of which he was the chairman proposed to give it up.

President both in the primary election by Electors and in the contingent election by the House of Representatives. The Eighth Congress and the states, in passing the Twelfth Amendment, extended the majority principle to the case of the Vice President. Madison, commenting in 1823 on a proposal identical with that of Senator Lodge, remarked: "The mode which you seem to approve, of making a *plurality* of electoral votes a definitive appointment would have the merit of avoiding the legislative agency in appointing the Executive; but might it not, by multiplying hopes and chances, stimulate intrigue and exertion, as well as incur too great a risk of success to a very inferior candidate? Next to the propriety of having a President the real choice of a majority of his constituents, it is desirable that he should inspire respect and acquiescence by qualifications not suffering too much by comparison." [8]

It is worth observing that these arguments would gain in force by the introduction of a system of proportional voting and the abolition of the intermediate Electors; for the former would tend to multiply the number of candidates, and the latter would make impossible the subsequent reduction of that number by the device of Electors voting their constituents' second choices. The leading candidate might have a very small proportion indeed of the popular or electoral vote. He might even be totally obnoxious to a great majority of the nation. As Madison stated to Henry Lee: "In what degree a plurality of votes is evidence of the will of the majority of voters, must depend on circumstances more easily estimated in a given case than susceptible of general definition. The greater the number of candidates among whom the votes

[8] Madison to George Hay, August 23, 1823 (Madison, *Writings*, IX, 153).

are divided, the more uncertain must, of course, be the inference from the plurality with respect to the majority." [9]

Fortunately it is not necessary to choose absolutely between a majority and a plurality system. Many reformers nowadays support what might be called the qualified plurality system. The so-called Lucas amendment, adopted by the Senate in 1950, as part of the abortive Lodge-Gossett resolution, will serve to illustrate it. That amendment would have made the primary election of the President the definitive election, provided that the number of electoral votes received by the leading candidate was equal to at least 40 per cent of the aggregate. Except in the unlikely case of a tie (for which it made a somewhat unsatisfactory provision), 213 votes out of 531 would, if a plurality, be sufficient to elect at the first trial.

The arguments in favor of such an amendment are two. In the first place, it would considerably reduce the chances of a failure in the primary election. This consideration would become of great importance if, as might possibly happen, given the present temper of the country, a strong sectional third party were to be established in the South. It would also become of importance if the general ticket system were to be broken up and a mode of voting adopted that would make easier the gaining of electoral votes, however few, by minor parties, sectional or national. Out of the past twenty elections, twelve may be characterized as close; in eight of them the victorious candidate received less than half the popular votes, and in the remaining four he received less than 52 per cent. It is apparent that in all of these the accidents of arithmetic under a different electoral voting system might have defeated the election. In the second place, the Lucas

[9] Madison to Henry Lee, January 14, 1825 (Madison, *Writings*, IX, 216).

amendment would not very greatly increase the risk of electing at the first trial a person who was not in any true sense the choice of the nation. Forty per cent is not an absolute majority, but as a relative majority, it may be thought a big enough share of the total to justify the drawing of inferences. Madison himself, as we have just seen, would have been willing to infer the will of the people from a relative majority of 33⅓ per cent.

The arguments against the Lucas amendment are mainly based on sentiment. We are told that the majority principle was dear to the Founding Fathers and is in some way fundamental to our institutions. It would appear, however, to have been peculiar to the New England states, and by them it was soon abandoned. Nowadays, no state chooses its Electors by the general ticket majority system, nor has anyone proposed that they do so. Nor has any reformer suggested that a district majority system be established. If the plurality principle is good enough for the appointment of Electors, perhaps, in a modified form, it will not be found intolerable for the appointment of the President.[10]

Other schemes have been proposed to keep the contingent election out of the House. In 1826 a committee of the Senate and a leading member of the House proposed that in case of a failure in the primary election, the two highest candidates should be referred back to the people voting directly for the President by districts.[11] Were the district plan to be established for the appointment of Electors, such a scheme might merit consideration. The objections to it, being chiefly temporal, could easily be overcome.

[10] The allegation that the Lucas amendment would promote the formation of third parties has been examined in another place; see pp. 165-166.

[11] II *Register of Debates*, 1366, 1378 ff., Appendix, pp. 121, 128-130.

More frequently, it has been suggested that in the event of a failure in the primary election, the Electoral College should be reconvened and required to choose a President from the two highest names on the list.[12] Such a proceeding would almost guarantee the election of a President at the second trial of the Electors, but it has never commanded much support. The arguments against it, though not altogether compelling, were sketched by Madison in 1824: "An appeal from an abortive ballot in the first meeting of the Electors to a reassembling of them, a part of the several plans, has something plausible, and, in comparison with the existing arrangement, might not be inadmissible. But it is not free from material objections. It relinquishes, particularly, the policy of the Constitution in allowing as little time as possible for the Electors to be known and tampered with. And beside the opportunities for intrigue furnished by the interval between the first and second meeting, the danger of having one electoral body played off against another, by artful misrepresentations rapidly transmitted, a danger not to be avoided, would be at least doubled. It is a fact within my own knowledge, that the equality of votes which threatened such mischief in 1801 was the result of false assurances dispatched at the critical moment to the Electors of one State, that the votes of another would be different from what they proved to be." [13]

[12] John Taylor of Caroline made such a proposal in the Senate, January 10, 1823 (40 *Annals*, 101). Cf. the Hayne amendment of December 15, 1823 (41 *Annals*, 39), the Van Buren amendment of December 29, 1823 (41 *Annals*, 74, 366), and the McDuffie Committee amendment of December 22, 1823 (41 *Annals*, 865, 1076). All these proposals looked forward to the inconclusive election of 1824.

[13] Madison to Jefferson, January 14, 1824 (Madison, *Writings*, IX, 174-175). Cf. Madison to McDuffie, January 3, 1824 (Madison, *Writings*, IX, 149n.).

Most reformers, however, would guard against the evils of the contingent election, not by avoiding a final resort to Congress, but by the substitution of a joint ballot of the members of Congress for a vote by states in the Representative branch. This was the mode approved by the Federal Convention when it contemplated allowing the national legislature to choose the President in the first instance. Its advantages are very apparent. It would make no change in the relative weights of the states between the first and second trials; it would exchange the federative for the popular principle in the making of the final choice; and by getting rid of the anomaly of divided ballots, it would make easier the reaching of a prompt decision.

It will be noticed that this plan of reform contemplates associating the Senators with the Representatives in the balloting for President, and some may inquire whether it might not be better to leave the choice solely to the Representatives voting by heads—as Representative Tucker is said to have suggested in 1819.[14] After all, the Representative branch is more nearly a political image of the people than Congress as a whole, and the person chosen would more certainly be in sympathy with the objects of the popular House. The answer is grounded on expediency. The small states are being asked to give up their equal vote in the contingent election; they are more likely to make the sacrifice if they are left the slight advantage accruing to them from their equal representation in the Senate.

The objections that have been made to changing the rule of voting in the contingent election are few and far-fetched. In 1826 Edward Everett of Massachusetts advanced the extraordinary doctrine that a constitutional amendment in-

[14] 34 *Annals*, 1420.

corporating such a change would itself be unconstitutional. Dividing the Constitution into its essential and unessential provisions, and distinguishing the power to amend from the power to alter, he suggested that the amending power could reach none of the federal features of the Constitution, among them the mode of electing the President. This argument would appear, however, to have been completely demolished at the time by Representative John S. Barbour of Virginia. Noticing that the article of the Constitution which provides for its own amendment contains a proviso that no state, without its consent, shall be deprived of its equal suffrage in the Senate, he opined that the interdict on the right of amendment reaches no farther: "The absurdity of prohibiting alteration in express words, of that most important Federative power, and leaving those of infinitely less moment, shielded in an equal degree, by implication only, would never have marked the deliberations of that august body of men who reared up our political fabric." [15]

Others have taken the position that a bargain is a bargain. In the Federal Convention it was anticipated that the election of the President would be managed in two stages. In the first stage the popular principle was to prevail; the sense of the people was to be tested in the nomination of candidates. If no candidate was favored by a majority of the people, then the names of the five most popular nominees were to be referred to the umpirage of the House of Representatives; but here the federative principle was to prevail; each state regardless of size was to have one vote. What was this but a compact between the states? Did not Madison call it "a compromise between the larger and smaller States, giving to the latter the advantage in selecting a President from the

[15] II *Register of Debates,* 1892-1893.

candidates, in consideration of the advantage possessed by the former in selecting the candidates from the people"? Let us take the very worst view of this compact. Let us admit that the present constitutional mode of choosing a President by the House of Representatives, when tested by the pure elective principle, must be deemed, as to the mode of choosing and the object of the choice, wholly exceptionable. Is a bad contract any less sacred than a good one? The large states were not deceived in the making of it. They gave up the popular principle in the eventual choice, not because they thought it was right to do so, but because the circumstances of the moment urged the concession. Are they now at liberty to take it back? Can the donor resume his gift without the consent of the donee?

These questions, and the answer they suggest, are very specious, but they take no account of the manner in which the large states have fulfilled their part of the federal compromise nor of the proposals that are actually being made to the small states. The popular principle, as we have already seen, was intended by the Constitution to give the election, or the nomination, of the President to the people in the nation at large; it was never meant to give it solely to the people of the large states. By consolidating their votes, however, the large states have, in effect, destroyed the popular principle and substituted for it a weighted federative principle. Every concession to the small states has been annihilated by the general ticket system; the extra votes accorded to them in the Electoral College are overbalanced by the impressed votes of the minorities in the large states; and the chance of influencing the contingent election comes to them but once in a century. Even then their range of selection has been reduced by the Twelfth Amendment, which confines them to a choice of three, instead of five. From a strictly legal point of view it might therefore be said that the federal compromise has already gone by the board and that a new and fairer arrangement might now very properly be negotiated.

Furthermore, the small states have little to lose and much to gain by surrendering a right that has long been reduced to nothing but an idea—"the cherished form of a lost substance," as it was once called by a committee of the Senate.[16] They are not being asked to give it up without an equivalent. For many years every proposal to change the rule of voting in the contingent election has been connected with a proposal to break up the consolidated voting system in the primary election. If the small states will resign their power to balance the great ones by their single votes in the House of Representatives, the great states will resign their power to overwhelm the small ones by their consolidated votes in the Electoral College. Both are being urged to yield something, not to each other, but to the people of the nation at large. Where is the danger to either? Would not both be infinitely safer if the popular principle were to operate at both stages of the election instead of at neither? If there be anything of concession here, beyond the mutually advantageous adjustments of a fair compromise, it is all on the side of the large states. "Of what advantage," asked a Senator from New Jersey in the days when that state was small, "is this power [of equal voting] to the small States, which has been exercised but once since the establishment of our Government, and was then considered as a great calamity? There can be none. What advantage can there be in retaining a power which it will be dangerous to exercise? None. Ambitious individuals in the small States may casually derive an importance from their situation, in the exercise of this power, but this can

[16] II *Register of Congress*, Appendix, p. 129.

be of no importance to the people of the States to which such individuals may belong. . . . What is this deadly blow aimed at the power of the small States? Simply a proposition that, if the large States will yield up the power by which they can completely suppress the voice of the small States in the first trial, on a Presidential election, the small States will so far give up their control in the last resort, as to choose a President by a joint vote of the two Houses of Congress; in which they reserve the extra power which the federative principle in our National Legislature gives them." [17] These remarks were made in March, 1824. The contingent election of 1825 went only to confirm them.

A few other objections have been made to the idea of per capita voting, but it seems scarcely worth while to disinter them. It has been said that every argument that can be urged in favor of taking from the small states their equal representation in the eventual election may be carried forward and urged with greater force in favor of depriving them of their true security, their equal representation in the Senate. But it may be answered that the Constitution itself precludes this possibility by giving to each state separately the power of vetoing such an alteration. It has been said that the power of choosing a President has been given to the House of Representatives alone, as an equipoise to the peculiar powers of the Senate in respect of treaties, appointments to office, and the trial of impeachments. But this objection cannot touch the rule of voting in the House. And if, under the new arrangement, the Senate would participate in the choice of the President, the House would participate in the choice of the Vice President.[18] It has been said that if the vote were taken per

---

[17] 41 *Annals*, 405, 406 (Senator Dickerson).

[18] Every resolution proposing to transfer the contingent election of the President from the House of Representatives to Congress pro-

capita, the influence of the Executive would be brought to bear upon the members of Congress. But would not this influence operate even more strongly if the vote were taken by states? The gaining of one member of the joint meeting would be no more than gaining one vote of 531; while the gaining of one member in the House of Representatives might be gaining one forty-eighth part of the whole. This would obviously be the case when a state had but one Representative; and it would also be the case when the representation of the state was so divided that a change of one individual vote would give the single state vote to one candidate instead of another, or prevent it from being given to anyone.

In summary, we must conclude that there is no valid objection to transferring the contingent election of the President from the House of Representatives, voting by states, to a joint meeting of Congress, voting by heads. On the contrary, there is every reason to do so.

There are some other matters that ought to be discussed in connection with any proposal to change the mode of determining the contingent election. From how many persons should the eventual choice be made? Should the Congress be required to choose not merely *immediately*, but without separation? Should the votes be given in by ballot or viva voce? If the result is to be determined by a majority of the individual votes of Congress, should that majority be of the combined authorized membership of the Senate and House of Representatives, or of the members present and casting significant votes?

With regard to the number of candidates, it is a question of three or two; for no one, it may be supposed, will wish to restore the number five, prescribed in the original Constitution,

poses also to transfer the contingent election of the Vice President from the Senate to Congress.

or advocate seven or thirteen, as did Sherman, Spaight, and Rutledge in the Federal Convention. Madison, in a letter to George Hay, set down the elements of the problem with his usual clarity: "It might be a question, whether the *three* instead of the *two* highest names might not be put within the choice of Congress, inasmuch as it not unfrequently happens, that the candidate third on the list of votes would in a question with either of the two first out-vote him, and, consequently, be the real preference of the voters. But this advantage of opening a wider door and a better chance to merit, may be outweighed by an increased difficulty in obtaining a prompt and quiet decision by Congress with three candidates before them, supported by three parties, no one of them making a majority of the whole." [19] Madison himself seems to have preferred the number two, for, in sketching a rather complicated process of his own invention, he would have had the final choice made by joint ballot of the House of Representatives and Senate out of the two or more names having the two highest numbers of votes on the list of those voted for as President by the Electors. [20]

Today the advantage of confining the choice to two persons is probably greater than in Madison's time. Then the election was to be made by the old Congress; now, by the new one. If a majority is to be found for one of three candidates, the supporters of one must sooner or later give up their man. But members who have been elected with direct reference to the presidential question are apt to be more intransigent than those who were chosen two years before, for the latter can always plead that the opinions of their constitu-

[19] Madison to George Hay, August 23, 1823 (Madison, *Writings*, IX, 152-153).

[20] *Ibid.*, p. 154; and Madison to McDuffie, January 3, 1824 (Madison, *Writings*, IX, 149n.).

ents have undergone a change and that their duty is to conform to it.

A proposal made in 1957 by Senators Mundt, Thurmond, Smith of New Jersey, and Mansfield is designed to secure the advantages both of "opening a wider door and a better chance to merit" and of "obtaining a prompt and quiet decision." For four ballotings three names would be before the House, but on the fifth the number would be reduced to two, namely the two obtaining the greatest number of votes on the fourth ballot. The suggestion is ingenious and merits consideration. It might be better, however, and more satisfactory to the people at large, to limit the choice on the fifth ballot to the persons having the two highest numbers of *electoral* votes. It is altogether too probable that the penultimate trial might be a false running, intended not to elect a President but to eliminate a candidate.

However this may be, it seems clear that, on balance, the advantages of choosing from two outweigh the advantages of choosing from three candidates. One difficulty remains to be noticed. It could sometimes happen that three or more persons might be tied with the highest number on the list, or that one person might have the highest and two or more persons be tied with the second highest numbers on the list. Some provision ought perhaps to be made in these cases "as well with a view to obviate uncertainty as to deal equally with equal pretensions." The ambiguous and clumsy language of the Twelfth Amendment—requiring the choice to be made "from the persons having the highest numbers not exceeding three on the list"—was intended to take care of such contingencies. Roger Griswold, explaining this language to the House of Representatives in 1803, spoke as follows: "I will venture to say three-fourths of the people who shall read it, will think that it is intended to confine the election to three persons; and yet, I understand, it is the intention of the Senate only to confine it to three classes. . . . The three highest numbers may refer to forty persons if they should be equal." [21] These remarks, it is true, contain some exaggeration. We are not to suppose that the House is compelled to extend its choice to "forty persons" if forty persons should have the three highest numbers. The phrase "not exceeding three" implies that the House may, if it chooses, confine the election to the persons having the *two* highest numbers or to the persons tied with the highest number.[22] If, for example, in 1825 the third and fourth candidates, Crawford and Clay, had been equally high in votes, the House might have admitted both or neither to the final contest.

In drafting an amendment to confine the choice of Congress to one of two persons it may seem the course of wisdom merely to change the word *three* in the Twelfth Amendment to *two*. But might it not be simpler, and productive of less difficulty, to go back to the wording of the original Constitution and substitute the word *two* for the word *five*—leaving Congress to choose "from the two highest on the list"? Perhaps, as Colonel Taylor suggested in 1803,[23] the difficulties to be apprehended from ties are imaginary. If two persons are tied with the highest number, there can be no advantage in an extension of the choice to the person or persons with the second highest number. If three or more persons are tied with the highest number, a choice from any two of them would be a correct choice; those least favored at the first trial could be eliminated in successive ballotings. If there were a tie for second place, it could be broken in the same way.

[21] 13 *Annals*, 677, 678.
[22] 13 *Annals*, 679 (Abraham Baldwin).
[23] 13 *Annals*, 93.

That the election should be *immediate* is a proposition that few will dispute. At this stage of the proceedings there can be no advantage in debate, and there should be no opportunity for filibuster. A committee of the House of Representatives, however, once suggested that the constitutional injunction of immediacy is not enough, and that the choice should be made *without separating*.[24] It is plain that the committee were looking back to the election of 1801. At that time it was decided that if the first balloting were inconclusive, the House would continue to ballot, without interruption of other business and without adjournment, until a President was chosen. The latter part of the rule was, however, upon experiment found impracticable and avoided afterwards by voting on one day that the next balloting should not take place until the next day. The result, as Daniel Webster later remarked, was "that all the members were, in fact, quietly sleeping in their beds, while the House, according to the journal and the rule, was all the time sitting." [25]

Asked by Representative McDuffie to comment on the committee's proposals in general, Madison took particular notice of this point. "Would it not be better," he wrote, "to retain the word 'immediately,' in requiring the two houses to proceed to the choice of President and Vice President, than to change it into 'without separating'? If the change could quicken and ensure a final ballot, it would certainly be a good one. But as it might give rise to disputes as to the validity of an election after an adjournment and separation forced by a repetition of abortive ballotings, the existing term might, perhaps, as well remain, and take its chance of answering the purpose. The distinction between a regulation which is directory only, and one a departure from which would have

[24] 41 *Annals*, 865.
[25] I *Register of Debates*, 433.

a vitiatory effect, is not always obvious; and in the delicate affair of electing a Chief Magistrate, it will be best to hazard as little as possible a discussion of it." [26] Madison's objections to changing the word *immediately* seem well taken; the House of Representatives itself appears to have viewed the matter in the same light, for, to govern the election of 1825, it adopted a rule permitting an adjournment if voted by a majority of all the states.

The Constitution says the House shall choose the President *by ballot*. A ballot, it will be recalled, is a secret vote. The name of a person is written on a piece of paper, and that paper is deposited, unsigned, in a ballot box. In the two elections that have been made by the House, this provision was scrupulously observed. No one can determine, by examining the journals of that body, how any individual member voted or how any state voted on any of the thirty-six ballotings of 1801 or on the single balloting of 1825. For 1801 the record shows only that for thirty-five ballotings the vote of the states stood eight for Jefferson, six for Burr, and two divided, and that on the final trial ten states voted for Jefferson, four for Burr, and two by blank ballots. For 1825 it shows only that thirteen states voted for Adams, seven for Jackson, and four for Crawford.

The procedure of the House, at both elections, was well calculated to preserve official secrecy. To begin with, each state delegation had to ascertain its own vote. To this end the Representatives from each state were seated together; they were provided with a ballot box; into this box each member dropped an unsigned ballot on which he had written either nothing or the name of the person whom he wished to make President; the box was then opened and the votes were

[26] Madison to McDuffie, January 3, 1824 (Madison, *Writings*, IX, 147-148n.).

counted; if it was found that an absolute majority of the members present and casting significant votes had concurred upon a single name, that name was written on the duplicate ballots that the state was later to give in; otherwise the word *divided* was written on those ballots; on these duplicate ballots the name of the state did not appear. The next order of business was to take up the state votes. Two general ballot boxes were provided; they were carried by the Sergeant at Arms to the several state delegations in turn; into each of them was deposited a duplicate of the state's vote; when the votes of all the states had been collected, the two boxes were taken to separate tables; tellers were appointed and divided into two groups; they counted the votes in each box and reported the results; the reports having been found in agreement, they were accepted as the true votes of the states.[27]

Speaking of this procedure in 1825, a member of the House emphasized its secrecy. "The Constitution," said Willie P. Mangum, "guaranties to us the mode of voting by *ballot*, in the exercise of which the vote of each delegation may be profoundly locked up in their own bosoms, and no human eye, not even the Argus eye of jealousy itself, can detect for whom the delegation voted. There are four States in the

[27] We may dismiss as fanciful the allegations of a pretended eye-witness that in 1825 the votes of the states were *not* put in general ballot boxes but were handed up one at a time to the tellers, proclaimed by the Vice President, and held aloft, written in large characters, so that the whole House could see them (Nathan Sargent, *Public Men and Events* [Philadelphia, 1875], I, 75-79). The scene described is obviously imagined. The Vice President, Daniel D. Tompkins, who is depicted by Sargent as presiding over the House of Representatives and, indeed, as occupying the Speaker's chair, was out of town. At the counting of the electoral votes his place had been taken by John Gaillard, President of the Senate, *pro tempore*; at the contingent election the presiding officer, who in no event could have been Tompkins, was Henry Clay, Speaker of the House.

Union represented in this House each by one member. Those gentlemen, according to the rules . . . , may hide their secret from all the world, if they choose. They have nothing to do but to make duplicate ballots, and drop one into each box, among twenty-three other votes, and how are their ballots to be known, to be identified?" [28]

Such is the law of the Constitution; it is very different from the practice. Unofficially, the vote of every member and, consequently, the vote of every state, is publicly known. In 1801 and in 1825 statements of the individual and state votes were printed in all the leading newspapers. No concealment was attempted or effected. In 1825 Louis McLane, the single member from Delaware, pointedly remarked: "Could there, indeed, be any concealment in the matter? Did not every member of this House know how his own colleagues intended to vote? And would he not disclose this knowledge?" [29] It is one thing to require secrecy and another to enforce it.

Of what value then are the words *by ballot?* Might it not be the part of common sense to strike them out of the Constitution and permit the votes of the individual members to be spread upon the record? Such a proposal could, indeed, be defended on theoretical grounds. A system of secret voting, it might be said, may be very desirable in a great popular election where bribery and intimidation are to be guarded against; but in Congress it should have no place. The elective franchise, when exercised by so small a group as 531 men out of 150 million, cannot be regarded as an individual right; it must be looked on as a trust. But a trust entails responsibil-

---

[28] I *Register of Debates,* 492. Delaware, Illinois, Mississippi, and Missouri were the four states referred to. They were represented by Louis McLane, Daniel P. Cook, Christopher Rankin, and John Scott, respectively.

[29] I *Register of Debates,* 429.

ity, and responsibility requires publicity. Every person in the United States is in the eyes of the Constitution a truster of the Congress; he is entitled to know and observe how his trustees have executed their trust. A constitutional provision that invites the members of Congress to treat as personal a right that belongs to their constituents ought, on theoretical grounds alone, to be struck from the sacred instrument.

It cannot even be said that the elimination of the words *by ballot* would introduce any new principle to our fundamental law; for, as that law now stands, the Senate in making the contingent choice of a Vice President is not now required to vote by ballot. In 1837, the sole occasion upon which it performed this duty, the Senators gave their votes viva voce, in their places on the call of the Secretary.[30]

It is worth noticing, however, that the secret vote can be abolished only by constitutional amendment. In 1825 an unsuccessful attempt was made to adopt a rule by which the vote of each state (but not the vote of each member) might be officially announced. It was answered, however, that such a rule would be in direct violation of the Constitution. "*Viva Voce,*" said Louis McLane, "might be a very good mode of voting for President, but, whether good or bad, was not now the question. It was not the mode which the Constitution had prescribed." [31]

One final question remains. Let it be supposed that a constitutional amendment is adopted transferring the con-

[30] In 1837 Richard M. Johnson, running for Vice President on the Van Buren ticket, failed to receive a majority of the electoral votes. The Virginia Electors had refused to support him. He was chosen by the Senate on February 8, the Virginia Senators voting for him. The purpose of the maneuver was apparently to register disapproval of his social behavior.

[31] I *Register of Debates,* 429.

tingent election from the House of Representatives voting by states to a joint meeting of Congress voting individually; and let it further be supposed that the range of persons from whom Congress may choose is limited to two. It is plain that the selection must be made by a majority vote. But ought it to be made by a majority of the combined authorized membership of both Houses rather than by a majority of the members present and casting significant votes? One cannot think so. A rule that permits absences and blank votes to affect the election would go a long way toward defeating the purpose of reducing the number of candidates to two; for when nonvotes and blank votes are counted in the total, they can prevent any candidate from obtaining a majority just as effectively as votes cast for a third person. The amendments currently being proposed usually require the more difficult majority; earlier amendments of the same type did not; and in the Federal Convention, when the details of the scheme of an original election by the legislature were worked out, it was decided, by a vote of 10 states to 1, that the choice should be by a majority of the votes of the members present.

The following language may be thought appropriate to a constitutional amendment designed generally to keep the election of the President out of Congress and particularly to change the mode of voting in Congress when the election does in fact devolve upon it. It would alter a part of the Twelfth Amendment:

> The President of the Senate shall, in the presence of the Senate and House of Representatives, open all the certificates, and the votes shall then be counted. The person having the greatest number of votes for President shall be the President, and the person having the greatest number of votes for Vice President shall be the Vice President, if such

number be at least 40 per centum of the whole number of Electors appointed. If on either list there are two who have such per centum and have an equal number of votes, then the Senate and House of Representatives, in joint meeting, shall immediately choose one of them for President or Vice President, as the case may be. If on either list no person shall have received votes equal to at least 40 per centum of the whole number of Electors appointed, then from the two highest on the list the Senate and House of Representatives shall, in like manner, choose the President or Vice President. In choosing the President or Vice President the votes shall be taken by heads and not by States, and a majority of the votes of whole number of Senators and Representatives present and voting shall be necessary to a choice.

A final observation may be in order. In working for an amendment of the existing system, reformers must bear in mind that they cannot dissociate the contingent election from the primary election. It is perfectly idle to talk of retaining the general ticket system and changing the mode of voting in Congress, or of keeping the latter and abolishing the former. The larger states will never part with the advantage they now have of moving in a solid, unbroken phalanx and giving to their favorite candidate an undivided electoral vote so long as the smaller states retain the contingent power of forcing their own candidate upon the country by their equal vote in the House of Representatives. Conversely, the smaller states will never surrender their contingent power to choose the President, so long as the larger states are able in the primary election to substitute their will for the will of the people of the nation as a whole. The only hope of reform lies in a double amendment—in the possibility envisaged by the reformers of long ago that the states of every size, certain of an ample equivalent, will consent to sacrifice their peculiar but unjust advantages on the altar of their common country.

Whether there is any real probability of reform at the present time is a question that may be left to the judgment of practical statesmen. It may be that nothing can be done until misfortune strikes—until there is a failure in the popular election and a choice by the House of Representatives of a President plainly obnoxious to a majority of the people. But in the meantime let those who debate the various plans of amendment remember that the powers mutually to be surrendered by the large and small states are not to be lost but vested in the people. And let them not forget the true character of the supposed conflict of interests between the large and small states involved in the entire proposal. In the words of Representative McDuffie, the great advocate of state rights, the supporter of Calhoun: "It is, in reality a contest, not between the large and the small states, but between the politicians, both of the large and the small States, on the one side, and the People of the United States on the other. Disguise it as we may, 'to this complexion it must come at last.'"

Appendix

I

PROVISIONS OF THE CONSTITUTION OF THE UNITED STATES GOVERNING THE ELECTION OF THE PRESIDENT AND VICE PRESIDENT

ARTICLE II, SECTION I. The executive Power shall be vested in a President of the United States of America. He shall hold his Office during the Term of four Years, and, together with the Vice President, chosen for the same Term, be elected, as follows

Each State shall appoint, in such Manner as the Legislature thereof may direct, a Number of Electors, equal to the whole Number of Senators and Representatives to which the State may be entitled in the Congress: but no Senator or Representative, or Person holding an Office of Trust or Profit under the United States, shall be appointed an Elector.

[The Electors shall meet in their respective States, and vote by Ballot for two Persons, of whom one at least shall not be an Inhabitant of the same State with themselves. And they shall make a List of all the Persons voted for, and of the Number of Votes for each; which List they shall sign and certify, and transmit sealed to the Seat of the Government of the United States, directed to the President of the Senate.

The President of the Senate shall, in the Presence of the Senate and House of Representatives, open all the Certificates, and the Votes shall then be counted. The Person having the greatest Number of Votes shall be the President, if such Number be a Majority of the whole Number of Electors appointed; and if there be more than one who have such Majority, and have an equal Number of Votes, then the House of Representatives shall immediately chuse by Ballot one of them for President; and if no Person have a Majority, then from the five highest on the List the said House shall in like Manner chuse the President. But in chusing the President, the Votes shall be taken by States, the Representation from each State having one Vote; A quorum for this Purpose shall consist of a Member or Members from two thirds of the States, and a Majority of all the States shall be necessary to a Choice. In every Case, after the Choice of the President, the Person having the greatest Number of Votes of the Electors shall be the Vice President. But if there should remain two or more who have equal Votes, the Senate shall chuse from them by Ballot the Vice President.] *

The Congress may determine the Time of chusing the Electors, and the Day on which they shall give their Votes; which Day shall be the same throughout the United States.

No Person except a natural born Citizen, or a Citizen of the United States, at the time of the Adoption of this Constitution, shall be eligible to the Office of President; neither shall any Person be eligible to that Office who shall not have attained to the Age of thirty five Years, and been fourteen Years a Resident within the United States. . . .

AMENDMENT XII. The Electors shall meet in their respective states, and vote by ballot for President and Vice-President, one of whom, at least, shall not be an inhabitant of the same state with themselves; they shall name in their

* This paragraph has been superseded by Amendment XII.

ballots the person voted for as President, and in distinct ballots the person voted for as Vice-President, and they shall make distinct lists of all persons voted for as President, and of all persons voted for as Vice-President, and of the number of votes for each, which lists they shall sign and certify, and transmit sealed to the seat of the government of the United States, directed to the President of the Senate;—The President of the Senate shall, in the presence of the Senate and House of Representatives, open all the certificates and the votes shall then be counted;—The person having the greatest number of votes for President, shall be the President, if such number be a majority of the whole number of Electors appointed; and if no person have such majority, then from the persons having the highest numbers not exceeding three on the list of those voted for as President, the House of Representatives shall choose immediately, by ballot, the President. But in choosing the President, the votes shall be taken by states, the representation from each state having one vote, a quorum for this purpose shall consist of a member or members from two-thirds of the states, and a majority of all the states shall be necessary to a choice. [And if the House of Representatives shall not choose a President whenever the right of choice shall devolve upon them, before the fourth day of March next following, then the Vice-President shall act as President, as in the case of the death or other constitutional disability of the President.] *
—The person having the greatest number of votes as Vice-President, shall be the Vice-President, if such number be a majority of the whole number of Electors appointed, and if no person have a majority, then from the two highest numbers on the list, the Senate shall choose the Vice-President; a quorum for the purpose shall consist of two-thirds of the whole number of Senators, and a majority of the whole number shall be necessary to a choice. But no person constitution-

* This part has been superseded by section 3 of Amendment XX.

ally ineligible to the office of President shall be eligible to that of Vice-President of the United States.

[*Proclaimed September 25, 1804, to be in force.*]

II

MODEL FOR AN AMENDMENT TO THE CONSTITUTION TO CHANGE THE METHOD OF ELECTING THE PRESIDENT AND THE VICE PRESIDENT

For the purpose of choosing a President and Vice President of the United States, each State shall be divided by the Legislature thereof into as many districts as will equal the number of Representatives to which such State may be entitled in Congress, and each district shall be composed of contiguous and compact territory and contain, as nearly as may be, the number of persons which entitles the State to a Representative in Congress according to the apportionment; which districts, when laid off, shall not be altered until after another census shall have been taken.

The inhabitants of each of the said districts, who shall have the qualifications requisite for electors of the most numerous branch of the State Legislature, shall choose one Elector of President and Vice President. The inhabitants of each State, having the same qualifications, shall choose two Electors of President and Vice President. But no Senator or Representative or person holding an office of trust or profit under the United States, shall be appointed an Elector.

The Electors shall meet in their respective States, and vote for President and Vice President, one of whom, at least, shall not be an inhabitant of the same State with themselves; they shall distinguish in their suffrages between the person voted for as President and the person voted for as Vice President, and they shall make distinct lists of all persons voted for as President and of all persons voted for as Vice President, and of the number of votes for each, which lists they shall sign and certify, and transmit sealed to the seat of government of the United States, directed to the President of the Senate.

The President of the Senate shall, in the presence of the Senate and House of Representatives, open all the certificates and the votes shall then be counted. The person having the greatest number of votes for President shall be the President, and the person having the greatest number of votes for Vice President shall be the Vice President, if such number be at least 40 per centum of the whole number of Electors appointed. If on either list there are two who have such per centum and have an equal number of votes, then the Senate and House of Representatives, in joint meeting, shall immediately choose one of them for President or Vice President, as the case may be. If on either list no person shall have received votes equal to at least 40 per centum of the whole number of Electors appointed, then from the two highest on the list the Senate and House of Representatives shall, in like manner, choose the President or Vice President. In choosing the President or Vice President the votes shall be taken by heads and not by States, and a majority of the votes of whole number of Senators and Representatives present and voting shall be necessary to a choice.

The places and manner of holding elections for Electors of President and Vice President shall be prescribed in each State by the Legislature thereof; but the Congress may at any time by law make or alter such regulations.

Index

Adams, John, 26, 32-34, 36, 174, 180

Adams, John Quincy, 38, 48, 52-53, 58, 76, 176, 177-179, 187, 188

Alabama, 77, 175, 182

Archer, William S., 140

Bagehot, Walter, 125-126

Baldwin, Abraham, 14, 21, 117, 204

Barbour, James, 100, 131, 175

Barbour, John S., 58n., 197

Bayard, James A., 32n., 58

Bedford, Gunning, 8

Benton, Thomas Hart, 62-63, 79n., 82, 91, 170, 171, 191n.

Blaine, James G., 102-103

Boudinot, Elias, 30

Brearley, David, 14

Broughton, Joseph M., 115

Bryan, John H., 21

Bryan, William Jennings, 74, 77

Buckalew, Charles R., 119-120

Burr, Aaron, 31, 32, 34-35, 183, 187

Butler, Pierce, 14, 38, 39n.

Cabot, George, 37, 38n.

Calhoun, John C., 188

California, 74, 75, 87-88, 182

Carroll, Daniel, 14, 20, 21

Cass, Lewis, 87

Clay, Henry, 52, 87, 178-179

Cleveland, Grover, 74, 75, 80

Clinton, De Witt, 23, 34, 48, 64, 183

Clinton, George, 40, 174

Clopton, John, 22

Cocke, William, 39

Colorado, 65

Committee of Eleven, of Federal Convention, 18-19

Connecticut, 97

contingent election, 184-212
   conditions governing, 184-187
   schemes to prevent, 191-200
   suggested changes, 201-211
   Twentieth Amendment and, 189-190

Cook, Daniel P., 208n.

219

Coudert, Frederic R., Jr., 152
Cragin, Aaron H., 104
Crawford, William H., 48, 51-52, 76, 177-179, 187, 188
Croker, Richard, 74n.

Dana, Samuel W., 24n.
Daniel-Mundt amendment, 104, 165
Dayton, Jonathan, 33n.
Delaware, 98
Dewey, Thomas E., 88
Dickerson, Mahlon, 46, 49n., 66n., 85, 90-91, 117n., 130, 138, 199-200
Dickinson, John, 14
disputed elections, 115-116
district system of electing Electors, 57-62, 66, 85, 92-93, 116, 128-168
Dixon, Robert G., Jr., 155-156
double voting system, by Electors, 24-41, 174
Douglas, Paul H., 145

Everett, Edward, 65, 137, 145, 196

faculty of change, 42-54, 78, 112, 133, 140-144
Federal Convention, 1787, 3-22, 191, 197, 202, 210
    Grand Committee (Committee of Eleven) on plan for choosing President, 13-17
    various modes of electing President, 6-13
"Federal Thirteen," or "Spartan Band," in Pennsylvania legislature, 50
Ferguson, Homer, 123
Fitzgerald v. Green, 45
Florida, 65, 86
Fourteenth Amendment to Constitution, 101-103, 149
Franklin, Benjamin, 25
Fromentin, Eligius, 53n.

Gaillard, John, 207n.
Gallatin, Albert, 58, 170
Garfield, James A., 74, 114, 147
Gaston, William, 60, 138, 146
general ticket plurality system of choosing Electors, 47-48, 57, 61, 62, 64-67, 71-94, 115-116, 123, 128-129, 139, 144-150
    arguments against, 78-94
    pressure groups and splinter parties in, 88-89
    split-ticket voting in, 73-77
geographic constituency, vs. voluntary constituency, 125-126
Gerry, Elbridge, 12, 21, 151, 180
gerrymandering, 149-159
Gilman, Nicholas, 14
Goodrich, Chauncey, 33, 36n.
Grant, Ulysses S., 86
Griswold, Roger, 41, 203
Grosvenor, Thomas P., 152, 160

Hamilton, Alexander, 19, 22, 23, 32, 58

Hammond, Jabez D., 53n., 142
Hancock, Winfield S., 74, 114, 147
Harrison, Benjamin, 74, 75, 77, 80, 87
Hartley, Thomas, 125
Hastings, Seth, 31n.
Hay, George, 85n., 128n., 185n., 191n., 202n.
Hayes, Rutherford B., 80, 86, 116
Hayne, Robert Y., 58, 195n.
Hendricks, Thomas A., 101n., 161
Henry, Patrick, 25
Hillhouse, James, 40
Hoffman, Michael, 43n., 57n.
Holland, James, 170, 182-183
Huger, Benjamin, 49
Hughes, Charles Evans, 74, 88

ideological groups of people, representation of, 117
"Immortal Seventeen," in New York Senate, 1824, 51-52

Jackson, Andrew, 48, 58, 76, 177-179, 181, 187, 188
Jackson, James, 31n.
Jay, John, 34
Jefferson, Thomas, 4, 31, 32-35, 36, 38, 40, 58, 60, 61, 143, 145, 170, 176, 177, 180, 183, 187, 195n.
Johnson, Magnus, 121n.
Johnson, R. M., 209n.

Kellogg, Charles, 170n.

Kennedy, John F., 140, 144, 145
King, Rufus, 14, 20, 21, 58, 94
Knox, Henry, 34n.

Lacock, Abner, 56, 97
Langer, William, 95
Lea-Walsh amendment, 120-121
Lee, Henry, 192, 193n.
Lee, Richard Henry, 23
legislative mode of electing Electors, 61-64
Lehman, Herbert H., 95
Lehman amendment, 95, 104
Lieber, Francis, 101-103
Lispenard, Anthony, 183
Lloyd, Thomas, 30n.
Lodge, Henry Cabot, Jr., 113, 115, 118, 191, 192
Lodge-Gossett amendment, 113, 115, 118-122, 165, 179, 193
and Maish amendment, 119-120
Louisiana, 77, 86
Lowndes, Thomas, 26n.
Lucas amendment, to Lodge-Gossett resolution, 165-166, 193-194

McDuffie, George, 47, 57, 58n., 60, 65, 79n., 83, 88n., 92-93, 133, 137, 139, 143, 185, 190, 205, 212
McKinley, William E., 77, 114
McLane, Louis, 208-209
McMaster, J. B., 177-179
Macon, Nathaniel, 58, 143

McPherson *v.* Blacker, 44

Madison, James, 6, 13, 14, 16, 19, 21-22, 24, 32, 48, 58, 61, 63, 64, 77*n.*, 84, 85, 90, 128, 135, 143, 180, 185*n.*, 191, 192, 194*n.*, 195, 197, 202

Maine, 98, 104

Maish amendment, and proportional voting, 119-120

Mangum, Willie P., 106*n.*, 207-208

Mansfield, Mike, 203

Marshall, John, 37, 84, 85

Maryland, 48, 62, 74, 75, 76, 187

Mason, George, 5, 7, 12, 17, 19, 23, 25, 184, 191

Mason, Jeremiah, 56, 99

Massachusetts, 46, 62, 151, 179-180

Michigan, 65, 78

Miles, Samuel, 74*n.*, 176

minorities, 88-90

Mississippi, 77, 175

Monroe, James, 32, 176

Morris, Gouverneur, 14

Mundt, Karl, 152-155, 203

Mundt-Coudert amendment, 152-155

Mundt-Thurmond-Smith-Mansfield amendment, 203

Murfree, William H., 56*n.*

national elections:
  1788, 34, 47, 73
  1792, 34, 45, 46, 173-174
  1796, 32-34, 36, 45, 61, 74, 75, 174, 176, 179-180, 180*n.*

national elections (Cont.)
  1800, 31-32, 35, 45, 49-50, 174, 183, 187, 206-208
  1804, 38, 40
  1808, 62
  1812, 48, 50-51, 60, 62, 63-64, 77
  1816, 62
  1820, 176
  1824, 47, 48, 51-52, 75-76, 177-179, 187, 206-208
  1828, 48
  1836, 64, 106*n.*, 209
  1844, 87-88
  1848, 87
  1856, 182
  1868, 65, 86
  1876, 65, 80, 86
  1880, 74, 114, 147
  1888, 80   [147
  1892, 65, 74, 74*n.*, 75, 76, 77,
  1896, 76, 77, 114
  1904, 74, 75
  1908, 74
  1912, 74, 75, 181, 182
  1916, 74, 87-88
  1948, 88, 162, 179, 182
  1952, 104
  1956, 139-140, 176

national plebiscite system, 56, 95-110
  effect of different state voting requirements on, 99-104
  need of constitutional amendment to establish, 97-99
  weaknesses of, 105-109

Negroes, representation of, 11, 15, 72, 149

Negroes, representation of (Cont.)
  effect of, on national plebiscite system, 88-90, 100-102, 109-110
Nevada, 98, 99, 112, 129n.
New Hampshire, 47, 48, 104
New Jersey, 48, 50-51, 62, 63
New York, 32, 46, 51-52, 54, 57, 73, 81, 82, 85, 86, 87, 99, 111, 112, 134, 135, 139, 152, 178-179, 183, 187
North Carolina, 45, 48, 63-64, 75, 173-174, 177, 179, 181
North Dakota, 74, 75, 153

Ohio, 74, 75, 77
Oklahoma, 97

Page, John, 25
Parker, Alton B., 74
Paterson, William, 14
Pennsylvania, 49-50, 62, 75, 82, 91, 153, 176, 177
Pickens, Israel, 49, 53n., 54, 60n., 90, 91
Pickering, Timothy, 3, 4, 20, 28, 38n.
Pinckney, Charles, 20, 43, 172, 176
Pinckney, Charles Cotesworth, 22, 32
Pinckney, Thomas, 33-34, 36
Plater, John R., 180n.
Plumer, William, 3, 27, 29n., 176
Poland, Luke P., 108
Polk, James K., 87, 143, 145
popular voting by districts for Electors, 57-59

Powell, Levin, 179
presidential Electors, 12-13, 14-16
  appointment of, 42-67
  abuses in, 49-52, 62
  reforms in, offered, 54-59
  usual methods of, 46-54
  methods of choosing, district system, 71-95
  general ticket system, 71-95
  legislative system, 61-64
proportional representation (P.R.), and proportional voting system, 117-127
proportional voting system, 111-127
  difficulties of, 115-118
  features of, 111-115

Randolph, Edmund, 19, 25
Randolph, John, 150-151
Rankin, Christopher, 208n.
Rhode Island, 98, 104
Roosevelt, Theodore, 74, 75, 181
Rutledge, John, 202

Saunders, Romulus, 48n., 64
Scott, John, 208n.
Sedgwick, Theodore, 32
Seymour, Horatio, 86
Sherman, John, 96
Sherman, Roger, 7, 14, 18, 202
single-member district system, 128-168
  arguments in favor of, 132-136

single-member district system (Cont.)

machinery for districting, 157-158

New Jersey Plan, 130-132, 139

objections to, 136-167

slaves, suffrage of, 11, 15

Smith, H. Alexander, 203

Smith, Samuel, 20

Smith, William, 36

South Carolina, 64-65, 75, 83, 86, 106, 112

South Dakota, 181

Spaight, Richard Dobbs, 202

splinter parties, 88-89

Storrs, Henry R., 43n., 52, 137

Taft, William Howard, 74, 181

Taylor, John, 39, 195n., 204

Taylor, Robert, 181n.

Taylor, Zachary, 87

Tennessee, 45-46, 179

Texas, 77

Thurmond, J. Strom, 162, 179, 203

Tilden, Samuel J., 80, 86

Tillman, George Dionysius, 106n.

Tompkins, Daniel D., 207n.

Tracy, Uriah, 29, 30, 35n.

Truman, Harry S, 88, 164, 179

Tucker, Henry St. George, 131, 196

Twelfth Amendment to Constitution, 23-41, 174, 184, 204, 210-211

Twentieth Amendment to Constitution, 189-190, 198

Van Buren, Martin, 52n., 58, 87, 195n.

Vermont, 98, 104, 187

Vice President, election of, 25-41

amendment dealing with, 36-41

difficulties of, 34-37

original plan, 30-31

Virginia, 61, 62, 84-85, 112, 153, 174, 179

voluntary constituency, vs. geographical constituency, 125-126

voters, varying qualifications of, effects of, 11, 56, 99, 103, 105-110

Wallace, Henry A., 88, 162

Walsh, David I., 120

Weaver, James B., 74, 147

Webster, Daniel, 58

Whipple, Thomas, Jr., 48n.

Williamson, Hugh, 11, 14, 191

Wilson, James, 3, 12, 20, 191

Wilson, Woodrow, 74, 88, 164, 181

Wolcott, Oliver, 32, 33, 36n., 174n.

Wolcott, Oliver, Jr., 32, 33

Wood *v.* Brown, 123

Wright, Silas, 87

Wyoming, 98

Yates, Joseph C., 54n.